ENCOUNTERING EDUCATION

ELEMENTS FOR A
MARXIST PEDAGOGY

ENCOUNTERING EDUCATION

ELEMENTS FOR A
MARXIST PEDAGOGY

Derek R. Ford

Published by *Iskra Books* 2022

Iskra Books
Madison, Wisconsin
U.S. | U.K. | Ireland | Canada | Australia | India
Iskra Books is the imprint of the *Center for Communist Studies*, an
international research center dedicated to the advancement of academic
and public scholarship in the fields of applied communist theory and
Marxist-Leninist studies.
ISBN-13: 978-1-0880-1258-1

British Library Cataloguing in Publication Data
A catalogue record for this book is available from the British Library

Library of Congress Cataloguing-in-Publication Data
A catalog record for this book is available from the Library of Congress

Cover Art by Sarah Pfohl
Cover Design and Typesetting by Ben Stahnke
Printed and Distributed by IngramSpark

CONTENTS

ACKNOWLEDGEMENTS

The elements assembled in this book have taken on various forms with different comrades and friends over the last few years. I want to thank my students Summer Pappachen, Maria Esposito, Meg Fosher, and Katie Swenson for thinking about wonder, stupidity, and sound with me. An early version of the first chapter appeared on *Liberation School* and benefitted from the insight of the editorial collective there. Tyson Lewis and Weili Zhao helped shape the second chapter, while Kiff Bamford helped with the third and Petar Jandrić and Curry Malott helped with the fourth. Different versions of chapters one, two, and four appeared in *Educational Philosophy and Theory*, *Studies in Philosophy and Education*, and *Postdigital Sciences and Education*, while a version of chapter three appeared in Kiff Bamford and Margret Grebowicz's *Lyotard and Critical Practice* through Bloomsbury. Thanks, finally, to the team at Iskra Books for their helpful comments and careful readings.

INTRODUCTION

MARXIST POLITICS, PHILOSOPHY, AND PEDAGOGY

It is common knowledge that Marx insisted philosophers should not just interpret the world but change it. Yet many forget, repress, or bypass (for various material and theoretical reasons) the *direction* toward which he wanted to change it, which was inextricably linked with *what* he studied and wrote—with marxist *theory*, in other words. Marx made this most explicit in a famous 1852 letter to Joseph Weydemeyer, a comrade who emigrated from Germany to the U.S. and fought in the Union Army against slavery.[1] In the letter, Marx writes that bourgeois theorists before him had discovered the existence of classes and the class struggle, but that what he proved was that the class struggle can lead to the dictatorship

---

1 Throughout this text and others, I don't capitalize "marxist" to draw our attention away from the individual Marx and toward the class struggle of which his work was an expression.

of the proletariat, and that the "dictatorship [of the proletariat] itself only constitutes the transition to the *abolition of all classes* and to a *classless society*."[2] In 1852 he hadn't, of course, discovered the concept that would theoretically arm our class in this struggle—surplus-value—but the project was consistent throughout his life. It's a project, however, that today some—including but not limited to marxist academics—have abandoned.

As such, it's helpful to begin with a lesson that Louis Althusser learned from Lenin, that what "a *'practice'* of philosophy, and the consciousness of what practicing philosophy" entails is "the consciousness of the ruthless, primary fact that philosophy *divides*."[3] The marxist tradition that orders practice above theory is often misunderstood because in marxism there is no harsh binary between the two—such a binary is *idealist*. Instead, marxist philosophy begins from everyday practices of production and reproduction or struggle and defeat, proceeds through conceptual abstraction, before returning to the real concrete with new thoughts that are hopefully more correct, which means they will advance the class struggle at a particular conjuncture.

The class struggle is, crucially, a fight against the capitalist mode of production and for the communist mode of produc-

---

2 Karl Marx, "Marx to Joseph Weydemeyer," in *Marx and Engels Collected Works (Vol. 39): Letters 1852-1855*, ed. J.S. Allen, P.S. Foner, D.J. Struik, and W.W. Weinstone (London: Lawrence & Wisehart, 1852/2010), 62-65.

3 Louis Althusser, *History and Imperialism: Writings, 1963-1986*, trans. G.M. Goshgarian (Cambridge: Polity Press, 2020), 13.

tion. Althusser tells us that Marx "never provided a true, concise, well thought-out definition of the mode of production."[4] Marx instead offered two definitions. In the chapter on the labor process, Marx tells us how to distinguish between the different modes: "It is not the articles made, but how they are made, and by what instruments."[5] In this definition, a mode of production is a way of producing articles of utility and is determined by the *means* of production. Yet later, Marx writes that production on an expanded scale "does not present itself as accumulation of capital, nor as the function of a capitalist, so long as the labourer's means of production, and with them, his product and means of subsistence, do not confront him in the shape of capital."[6] Here the mode of production refers to "the *way of* producing in the social sense," which is "*the whole process of production and reproduction*."[7] Put another way, a mode of production is about the means of production and the *relations* of production; both of which constitute the economic "base" of society. The relations of production are who produces, under what conditions, and how they relate to each other and—under capitalism—how they relate to those who do not produce but own. A mode of production, then, is not defined by legal or technical relations (even if it's par-

4 Althusser, *History and Imperialism*, 67.

5 Karl Marx, *Capital: A Critique of Political Economy (Vol. 1): The Process of Capitalist Production*, trans. S. Moore and E. Aveling (New York: International Publishers, 1867/1967), 175.

6 Ibid., 560.

7 Althusser, *History and Imperialism*, 68.

tially maintained through them) and is instead the unity of both the means and relations of production but—and this is an important but—"*under the dominance* of the relations of production."[8]

For Marx, the capitalist mode of production became dominant once it passed from formal subjection to real subjection. Capital at first merely takes the labor processes of handicraft and manufacture as it finds them (in England) and takes command over them by, for example, lengthening the working day. At this point capital has not yet acquired the direct control of the labour process insofar as the regulating mechanism of production is the worker who necessarily "maintains some autonomy from capital."[9] Real subjection takes place when "industries that have been taken over" by capital "continue to be revolutionised by changes in the methods of production."[10] Real subjection takes place when capital replaces living labor as the motor of production with dead labor, or machinery. As a result, capital's command over labor increases and intensifies, as the knowledge of the production process is objectified in machinery and technology and withheld from our class through the state's repressive apparatuses. Here, we see the two definitions of the mode of production in their unity: the means of production and the relations of production define capitalism, which comes into its own through real subjection.

---

8 Ibid., 69.

9 Curry Malott, "Capitalism, Crisis, and Educational Struggle in the Postdigital," *Postdigital Science and Education* 1, no. 2 (2019): 376.

10 Marx, *Capital (Vol. 1)*, 478.

Machinery, once it fully replaces the workers' tools, transforms the worker "into a fragment of a man," and "degrade[s] him to the level of an appendage of a machine."[11] Thus, not only the *relations* of production are changed but so too is the *subjectivity* of workers. At the same time, however, the figure of the *collective worker* is solidified. Guido Starosta goes so far as to claim that "large-scale industry begets, as its most genuine product, a *universal worker*, that is, a productive subject capable of taking part in any form of the human labour-process."[12] There is, as such, a contradictory process of subjectivation happening in which workers are both atomized and subjected to machinery while at the same time uniting to form a class. Our class is, in turn, constantly decomposed and recomposed through the *absolute general* law of capitalism, the result of which is a dynamic and ever-expanding industrial reserve army produced through technological developments.[13]

The industrial factory is thus a dialectical sublation, which is especially apparent given that it is precisely the *proletarians'* skills and knowledges that are objectified in machinery. The

11 Ibid., 604.

12 Guido Starosta, "The System of Machinery and Determinations of Revolutionary Subjectivity in the *Grundrisse* and *Capital*," in *In Marx's Laboratory: Critical Interpretations of the Grundrisse*, ed. R. Bellofiore, G. Starosta, and P.D. Thomas (Rotterdam: Brill, 2013), 239.

13 This is distinguished from the "absolute law" of capitalist accumulation, which is the production of surplus value. Further, it is "*like all other laws*... modified in its working by many circumstances." See Marx, *Capital (Vol. 1)*, 603, emphasis added.

proletarian, however, constitutes anyone subjected to capital, whether they're employed or not, whether they work for a wage or not, whether they produce a good or a service, whether they are in the city or the countryside, or the Global North or South. While at one point in *Capital* Marx defines the "productive worker" as one directly engaged in producing surplus value—and says it is a "misfortune," he later writes that "the maintenance and reproduction of the working-class is, and must ever be, a necessary condition to the reproduction of capital."[14] Surplus value is not just produced but has to be transported, exchanged, and realized or consumed. Proletarian is both an adjective and a verb, it's a *process*: the proletarianization of increasing numbers of people and communities, states, and nations, is precisely the process of capitalist production.

Wherever one falls in the ongoing process of proletarianization, one is part of this class from which capital expropriates land, subjectivity, knowledges, and skills.[15] One of the most interesting and potent examples is the cotton gin, an invention credited to Eli Whitney, something of a folk hero in the U.S. elementary school curriculum. Sam Marcy, however, argues that "the first gin made in Mississippi was constructed based on a crude drawing by a skilled slave," and becase "the slaves were never recognized in law as persons, the slave owners could appropriate their property as well as any inventions

14 Marx, *Capital (Vol. 1)*, 477, 537.

15 It's worth emphasizing that Marx noted that workers' lives are made "*the more precarious*" as a result of proletarianization, so the figure of the 'precariat' is nothing new. See Ibid., 603.

they might conceive of."[16] The impetus for the invention was the increased demand for cotton in England as a result of the industrial revolution. Capitalism intensified the barbarism of slavery and immiserated the English proletariat at the same time. Even under capitalism, in which the "individual" enters into a "contract" with a capitalist as free equals in juridical terms, proletarian knowledge forms key ingredients or blueprints for "capital's" technological transformations.

Here we see a rich dialectic unfold devoid of any traces of technological determinism. In his latest book, Andy Merrifield extrapolates on the fourth footnote in the chapter on machinery and modern industry in *Capital*, where Marx articulates his dialectical and historical-materialist approach to technology. "Humans make machines," he begins, "develop technology from bright ideas," which, in turn:

> emerge out of prevailing material circumstances. Yet as soon as those bright ideas are realized materially, get embodied in new technology, in new machinery, they react, help shape us in dramatically ambivalent ways. We make technology; technology remakes us. Technology changes prevailing ideas, too, which then open further possibilities for the development of other new ideas and add other new technological advancements.[17]

---

16 Sam Marcy, *High Tech, Low Pay: A Marxist Analysis of the Changing Character of the Working Class* (New York: World View Forum, 2009), 59.

17 Andy Merrifield, *Marx Dead and Alive: Reading* Capital *in Precarious Times* (New York: Monthly Review Press, 2020), 63.

The questions, of course, are whether and on what grounds these are technological *advancements* or merely technological *changes*. Yet the point stands: ideas, social relations, the mode of production, and the means of production exist in a dialectical relationship, with each impacting the others. This is consistent with marxist theory, that philosophy cannot be understood without historical, political, sociological, economic, and other forms of inquiry and practice, including education and pedagogy. [18]

Much marxist educational theory has primarily concerned itself with critiquing the structures, systems, and curricula of schooling rather than delving deeply into educational philosophy and pedagogy. The former concerns the *content* of education while pedagogy concerns the *relation* to the content; or the former concerns the *what* while the latter concerns the *how*. Of course, it is necessary to have an adequate political and ideological framework to engage in marxist education; yet this alone is insufficient. Pedagogy—as an educational methodology—has to be held in tension with political commitments. Both, of course, are guided by the practical concerns of the workers' movement historically and today, as well as by their potential future trajectories, potential trajectories that are immanent in the present.

It is this task which the essays in this book attempt to pursue. What this book is concerned with, to put it differently, is the articulation of the political contexts and the peda-

---

18 Karl Marx and Friedrich Engels, *The German Ideology: Part One, with Selections from Parts Two and Three and Supplementary Texts*, trans. C.J. Arthur (New York: International Publishers, 1932/1970).

gogical philosophies and practices of marxist education. The navigation between the two tasks is premised on what might be the most general marxist philosophy of education there is: the presumption of competence. Marxism is a theory for understanding and intervening in the world and is accordingly predicated on the ability of the working and oppressed classes to not only understand the world but take the power necessary to transform it in a communist direction. This is why Marx, Engels, Lenin, and others constantly decried socialists who "belittled" or "talked down" to workers.[19] If one does not think the masses are capable of knowing and acting, then why engage in revolutionary struggle at all?

Elements for Marxist Pedagogy

Interestingly, in the index of International Publishers edition of the first volume of Marx's *Capital*—the edition and translation prepared and approved by Progress Publishers, one of the Communist Party of the Soviet Union's publishing houses—there are no pages dedicated to the entry "mode of production." The index entry for "mode of production" points

---

19 See Karl Marx and Friedrich Engels, "Marx and Engels to August Bebel, Wilhelm Liebknecht, Wilhelm Bracke and Others (Circular Letter)," trans. P. Ross and B. Ross, in *Marx and Engels Collected Works (Vol. 45): Letters 1874-79*, ed. J.S. Allen, P.S. Foner, D.J. Struik, and W.W. Weinstone (London: Lawrence & Wisehart, 1879/2010); V.I. Lenin, "What is to be Done?" in *Essential Works of Lenin*, ed. H.M. Christman (New York: Dover Publications, 1987); and for more on Lyotard and the communist project, see Derek R. Ford, *Communist Study: Education for the Commons*, 2nd. ed. (Lanham: Lexington Books, 2021), 121-134.

you to "socio-economic formation." My speculation is that they wanted first to underscore that any mode of production is not just economic but social, but moreover to emphasize—as Marx did—that every socio-economic formation consisted of multiple modes of production. In the preface to the first German edition of *Capital*, for example, Marx justified his focus on England on the basis that it was where the capitalist mode of production was most developed but noted that "alongside of modern evils" of capitalism, "a whole series of inherited evils oppress us, arising from the passive survival of antiquated modes of production."[20] In fact, the very first sentence of the book contains a key qualifier that's often glossed over. "The wealth of those societies," Marx writes, "in which the capitalist mode of production *prevails*, presents itself as 'an immense accumulation of commodities.'"[21] While it's often noted that wealth *is not* commodities but only *appears* as such, what is less remarked is that the capitalist mode of production only *prevails*; it is not *exclusive*.

Even capitalism, for Marx, was not universalizing or totalizing. Marx saw capitalism as "housing" "a vast, heterogeneous inventory and 'conjuncture' of temporalities no longer stigmatized for having been cast out of time but rather as expressions of contretemps, simultaneous nonsimultaneities… contemporaneous noncontemporaneities or uneven times,

---

20 Marx, *Capital (Vol. 1)*, 20.

43, emphasis added.

and *zeitwidrig*, time's turmoil, times out of joint."[22] Nothing perhaps reveals Marx's temporal openness more than his suggestion that surviving communes in 19th century Russia were *progressive* relative to capitalism. Particularly in the *Grundrisse*, Marx "rejected any linear causality that envisaged a singularly progressive movement from one period or mode of production to the next… but rather saw the multilinear movements as taking place in different regions and among diverse peoples."[23] Thinkers in the Global South and elsewhere latched onto and developed such insights. To give just one example, Mariátegui's historical account of Peru accounted for indigenous communities, forms of common ownership or cultivation, Spanish colonial feudalism, and a republican capitalism. This was made possible exactly "because Marxism was open to diverse regional historical experiences that historical materialism had to account for, instead of remaining narrowly constrained by a singular and singularizing dogmatic discourse applied to all situations."[24] Unfortunately, Western marxism, including educational marxism, has often neglected Marx's complex conception of time and history. It is within such a heterogeneous complex of any given social formation that a new mode of production can arise.

I see the pedagogy that advances the class struggle in our social formation as a pedagogy of the encounter. Capitalism

22 Harry Harootunian, *Marx After Marx: History and Time in the Expansion of Capitalism* (New York: Columbia University Press, 2015), 23.

23 Ibid., 48.

24 Ibid., 140.

itself, after all, "sprung from a *historic 'encounter'*" between the capitalist and the wage worker and "the proof is that it is highly likely… *that the capitalist mode of production was born and died several times in history* before becoming viable."[25] Perhaps the first place to begin, then, is with Althusser, who always found Marx's work a rich source for study precisely *as a result of* its openness, its silences, its doubleness, and its contingency. While this is most explicit in his writing on the encounter, G.M. Goshgarian has shown that it's a continual theme from his first book, *For Marx*. It's in his posthumously published manuscript, "The Underground Current of the Materialism of the Encounter," however, where it is explored in most length.[26] Althusser begins the piece like Lucretius Carus who, writing about Epicurus, produced the poem "On the Nature of Things," which "says that, before the beginning of the world, the atoms were '*falling like rain*'. This would have gone on indefinitely, had the atoms not been endowed with an astonishing property, '*declination*', the capacity to deviate from the straight line of their fall."[27] Althusser begins his piece on the encounter by writing, "It is raining. Let this book therefore

---

25 Louis Althusser, *Philosophy for Non-Philosophers*, trans. G.M. Goshgarian (London: Bloomsbury, 2017), 134, 135, emphasis in original.

26 G.M. Goshgarian, "The Void of the Forms of Historicity as Such," *Rethinking Marxism* 31, no. 3 (2019): 243-272.

27 Althusser, *Philosophy for Non-Philosophers*, 29, emphasis in original.

be, before all else, a book about ordinary rain."[28] The materialism of the encounter is a historical materialism, a kind of riff on Marx and Engels' own, one that is true to their lineage in that it privileges contingency over necessity, chance over predictability.

Atoms fell parallel until there was a *swerve*, a *clinamen*, or "the *slightest 'deviance'* being "enough for the atoms to *encounter each other* and agglomerate."[29] For Epicurus, it is not that before the world there was nothing; in fact, before the world there was *something*: materiality. Yet the encountering—and more precisely, the piling up of encounters, the "taking hold" of enough encounters, produces a historic event. The atoms clashed, and enough encounters took hold that they created a world.

There is no reason to explore any origins; just the fact that the swerve happened. Each element itself is autonomous and conjunctural, which is why they "'conjoin' by 'taking hold' in a new structure."[30] The communist revolution is such a piling up of encounters of elements that "exist in history *in a 'floating' state* prior to their 'accumulation and 'combination.'"[31] "The forms in which communist elements appear in capitalist society," Althusser writes elsewhere, "are countless. Marx himself names a whole series of them, from forms of children's edu-

---

28 Louis Althusser, *Philosophy of the Encounter: Later Writings, 1978-1987*, trans. G.M. Goshgarian (New York: Verso, 2006), 167.

29 Althusser, *Philosophy for Non-Philosophers*, 29.

30 Althusser, *History and Imperialism*, 33.

31 Louis Althusser, *Philosophy of the Encounter*, 198.

cation combining work and schooling," "the proletarian community of life and struggle," "joint-stock companies," and so
on, to say nothing of the 'socialization of production.'"[32] Yet
these are "elements *for* communism," elements that communism will sublate, modify, adapt, and so on. There is no guar-
antee they will take hold, but particular pedagogical forms and
practices might help them do so.

The pedagogical encounter is "an exposure to an outside," and an excess or surplus *gap* within the lesson. As a
result, pedagogical encounters cannot "be brought about by
learning theory or the expertise of the teacher," but "rather
happen when a certain configuration of institutional and ex-
trainstitutional forces come into play."[33] For Tyson E. Lewis,
the educational space of the encounter is the seminar, which
allows for "a moment of disinterpellation through which students, materials (books, essays, films, and so forth), and the
teacher enter into a constellation of forces that destabilize
and thus open up a space and a time wherein a new kind of
educational life beyond the subject temporarily forms."[34] The
seminar is where teachers, students, and objects take up and
produce spaces—sonically, visually, kinesthetically. Whereas
interpellation brings the subject into the existing world and
counterinterpellation pushes back against that world, disinterpellation suspends and opens the world, allowing for the

32 Althusser, *History and Imperialism*, 64.

33 Tyson E. Lewis, "A Marxist Education of the Encounter:
Althusser, Interpellation, and the Seminar," *Rethinking Marxism* 29,
no. 2 (2017): 314.

34 Ibid., 316.

encounter. Disinterpellation "makes the subject unfamiliar to itself and thus open to its own dissolution through the encounter with an outside. Since the swerve of the encounter is never predictable and never reducible to the logic of learning a specific lesson of the teacher."[35]

There is no lesson learned nor is any lesson taught. Rather than the transmission of *knowledge* there's the transmission of *affects*. "The origin of transmitted affects," Teresa Brennan remarks, "is social in that these affects do not only arise within a particular person but also come via an interaction with other people and an environment. By the transmission of affect, I mean simply that the emotions or affects of one person, and the enhancing or depressing energies these affects entail, can enter into another."[36] As an affective experience, disinterpellation disobeys the boundaries between the abstracted included and excluded subjects of education, allowing us to encounter elements that can work against the abstraction of capitalism and help us experience the communist future in the present so that we may work toward creating more encounters and, ultimately, a revolutionary rupture.

The entire marxist project is to work towards the building up of encounters and differentializations by advancing the class struggle to establish the dictatorship of the proletariat and ultimately create a classless society without capitalist abstraction. As Marx and Engels tell us in *The German Ideology*, "communism is for us not a *state of affairs* which is to be es-

---

35 Ibid., 317.

36 Teresa Brennan, *The Transmission of Affect* (Ithaca: Cornell University Press, 2004), 3.

tablished, an *ideal* to which reality [will] have to adjust itself," and is instead "the *real* movement which abolishes the present state of this." Moreover, "the conditions of this movement result from the premises now in existence."[37] In sum, the pages that follow enunciate the premises now in existence and propose pedagogical responses for assembling such encounters so that, with the guidance of working-class organization, they can take hold, as they have started to with such tremendous (and detrimental) results in the past.

---

37 Karl Marx and Friedrich Engels, *The German Ideology: Part One, with Selections from Parts Two and Three and Supplementary Texts*, trans. C.J. Arthur (New York: International Publishers, 1970), 56-57.

1
_____

MARX'S PEDAGOGICAL CONSTELLATION: INQUIRY AND PRESENTATION

While Marx considered education at times, he never explicitly addressed pedagogy. One possible exception is in the 1872 preface to the French edition of *Capital*, which was to be published in serial format. Marx is fearful "that the French public... eager to know the connexion between general principles and the immediate questions that have aroused their passions, may be disheartened because they will be unable to move on at once."[1] The pedagogical problem concerns the unity of theory and practice, and Marx does not pose a pedagogical response, but a pedagogical warning: "There is no royal road to science, and only those who do not dread the fatiguing climb of its steep paths have a chance of gaining its luminous sum-

_____

1 Marx, *Capital (Vol. 1)*, 30.

mits."[2] As Tyson Lewis argues, this is ultimately a non-answer, as "the difficult labor of the concept [pedagogy] is largely left to the intellectual labor of the workers themselves."[3] Following Althusser, Lewis argues that there's a lag between marxist philosophy and marxist pedagogy.

Yet Marx actually poses a pedagogical framework the very next year, in his 1873 afterword to the second German edition of *Capital*, where he distinguishes the *Forschung* from the *Darstellung*, or the method of inquiry from that of presentation. Here Marx is responding to an assessment of *Capital* that appeared in an 1872 edition of the *European Messenger* based in St. Petersburg. The assessment focuses on Marx's method of presentation and commends Marx for showing the laws of capitalism and of social transformation. Marx claims this is ultimately an affirmation of his anti-Hegelian dialectic, but before clarifying his dialectic, he briefly notes the necessary differences between inquiry and formulation, a difference I take as pedagogical. "Of course," Marx writes, "the method of presentation must differ in form from that of inquiry." Inquiry, or studying, "has to appropriate the material in detail, to analyse its different forms of development, to trace out their inner connexion." The method of presentation, or learning, occurs only after this is accomplished. "Only after this work is done," he says, "can the actual movement be adequately

---

2 Tyson Lewis, "The Pedagogical Unconscious: Rethinking Marxist Pedagogy through Louis Althusser and Fredric Jameson," *Journal for Critical Education Policy Studies* 3, no. 2 (2005): 145.

3 Ibid.

described."[4] I think Marx is describing two different pedagogies—or educational processes or logics—here. In particular, the method of inquiry (or research) is akin to studying while the method of presentation is akin to learning.

Learning is guided by pre-determined ends, upholds binary distinctions between ignorance and intelligence, amateurism and professionalism, students and teachers, and so on. Learning is a developmental process that moves from the former to the latter by various means (constructivist, student-centered, dialogical, etc.). It is about the actualization of a pre-existing potential. Only on this basis can learning be measured, quantified, and assessed. Learning is attached to productivity, to "immediate utility in daily life," and "is more or less a linear process that unfolds chronologically toward maximum outputs."[5] The ontology of learning is the endless progression from impotentiality to potentiality, or from the state of "I cannot" to "I can."[6] Marx, indeed, wanted readers to *learn* from his presentation about the dynamics of capital, its contradictions, histories, potential futures, and fault lines to better intervene in the class struggle.

Studying, on the other hand, encompasses various practices that interrupt, delay, and deactivate learning. While studying, one might have a pre-determined end goal in mind, but that

4 Marx, *Capital (Vol. 1)*, 28.

5 Tyson E. Lewis and Daniel Friedrich, "Educational States of Suspension," *Educational Philosophy and Theory* 48, no. 3 (2016): 237, 238.

6 See Tyson E. Lewis, *On Study: Giorgio Agamben and Educational Potentiality* (New York: Routledge, 2013).

is quickly suspended as the studier finds themselves lost, wandering, and straying in unpredictable and unforeseeable ways. In essence, studying is a pedagogical style that renders existing and foreordained ways of being inoperative and, by doing so, it opens up the possibilities of what can be as the dictates of what *is* are suspended. As one example, Lewis and Friedrich propose tinkering as a form of studying. While tinkering, the student frees an object or process from any foreordained ends and "the instrumentality" of learning "and the success conditions determining proper vs. improper, success vs. failure are suspended indefinitely."[7] Or, as Weili Zhao succinctly phrases it, the "studier is supposed to forget-suspend its presuppositions and identities, ready to be ex-posed to some signatures hidden sporadically between the lines, evoked to what is unsaid or unresolved aporia, and/or provoked to elaborate the unsaid/aporia toward generating new possibilities."[8] The ontology of studying, to phrase it differently, is a fluctuation between the two states, an immersion in suspension between different methods, sources, and potential outcomes.

The method of inquiry is one that examines material in all of its nuances and relationships, tracing out the different lineages, past, present, and future potential forms of development, and how they each interdepend on and transform each other. As Marx put it in his 1857 Introduction, you move

---

7 Lewis and Friedrich, "Educational States of Suspension," 240.

8 Weili Zhao, "Calibrating *Study* and *Learning* as Hermeneutic Principles through Greco-Christian Seeing, Rabbinic Hearing, and Chinese *Yijing* Observing," *Studies in Philosophy and Education* 39, no. 3 (2020): 322.

from the world as it is—in our "chaotic conception… of the whole" to transition "from the imagined concrete towards ever thinner abstractions." Yet "from there the journey would have to be retraced" so that the world in its concreteness is "a rich totality of many determinations and relations."[9] This is the pedagogy of *inquiry* or studying. Such a pedagogy entails wandering around, looking for connections, developing and proposing abstractions and determinations, thinking you are onto something and then following it to a dead end, generating ideas, getting lost in the archives (or on YouTube or the internet), journeying out and wandering or *wondering* around. When Marx was studying, he had an end in mind: he wanted to understand the inner logics and dynamics of capital, how these came to be, what impact they had and might have on the world, and how the contradictions can be seized upon during the class struggle.

Only once you've adequately done this can you turn to *presenting* your findings. The presentation takes a totally different form. It begins with conceptual building blocks and proceeds linearly in a developmental manner. This is why Marx, in *Capital*, often casts aside the historical origins of British capital, the question of rent and finance, and so on. On first glance, it seems that *Capital* is exclusively a pedagogy of *learning* that begins with something simple and obvious (the commodity) and then goes deeper and deeper until we see that this "trivial" appearing thing is a series of ongoing struggles: be-

---

9 Karl Marx, *Grundrisse: Foundations of the Critique of Political Economy (Rough Draft)*, trans. M. Nicolaus (New York: Penguin, 1939/1993), 100.

and within classes and the state that play out differently over history, that assume different forms (like technology and machinery), and so on. But first, we have to get the concept of surplus-value before any of this makes sense, and in order to do that, we have to get to the basics of commodities, their two-fold nature, circulation, money, and so on. Learning or presentation is a developmental process that is more or less linear, advancing from the partial to the complete so that if "done successfully... it may appear as if we had before us a mere a priori construction."[10]

While Marx insists that only after studying is completed can the work be presented, this does not mean that the two pedagogies are linearly joined, so that studying must lead to learning. Yet the opposition is not as clear-cut as he makes it appear in the afterword. Ultimately, it is only after learning to read a text that one can study it; meanwhile, studying leaves *traces* in the product of learning. Both learning and studying are heterogeneously blocked together, and the task of marxist education is to facilitate the movement between the two. While Marx wanted workers to learn from his presentation, he knew he could not finish such a project, as no one can fully delineate and learn about capitalism so long as it exists, as capital is by definition a dynamic social relation. Andy Merrifield's recent reading of *Capital* seems to affirm this. Merrifield writes that "Marx never wanted to finish *Capital* because he could not see how it could ever be finished. He sought the definitive but knew the impossibility of the definitive. It

---

10 Marx, *Capital (Vol. 1)*, 28.

tormented him."[11] Indeed, when one reads the various out-lines that Marx presented for *Capital* in the *Grundrisse* and else-where, it is clear that Marx was taking on a project he knew he could never finish.

He wanted to write volumes on the state, the world mar-ket, foreign trade, wages, the history of theory, and more. Even in the first volume of *Capital*, we see traces of Marx's interminable studying in the various places he notes an abso-lutely crucial point—one we *must* understand—only to move on and say he cannot address it here and it will have to wait until later, until he's returned to studying. Sometimes, like when he brings up credit and rent in volume 1, he does return in volume 3. But other times, like when he brings up violations of the ideal law of exchanges, he never goes back, because, *as a pedagogical* text, *Capital* is more developmental.

As a result, Marx's pedagogies of learning and studying should be seen as *constellations*. Drawing on Walter Benjamin, Lewis maps out educational marxisms and contends that we should neither defend one at the expense of another nor put them as dots on a timeline unfolding into a completed dialec-tic synthesis or "final Marxist 'solution.'" Instead, he argues we should approach them as constellations, which do not "re-solve tensions within and between competing theories" and instead finds "that such tensions are productive indexes that both connect and disconnect singular theoretical registers."[12] Marx's pedagogical methods—deployed while writing and re-

11 Merrifield, *Marx Dead and Alive*, 15.

12 Tyson E. Lewis, "Mapping the Constellation of Educational Marxism(s)," *Educational Philosophy and Theory* 44, no. s1: 99.

searching—are best viewed in this way, as "hang[ing] precariously together, maintaining an absent center."[13] It is not that one subsumes the other or that they eventually transcend their differences in unity.

There is a dialectical relationship between inquiry and presentation. It may be that the relationship between the two is ultimately contingent upon a variety of factors, from the dominant mode of production to the state of the class struggle. In fact, as Althusser writes, Marx was only able to write *Capital* owing to his own experiences in the workers' movement. Marx claimed he wasn't a marxist to reject "the idea, 'obvious' to everyone at the time, that he, the individual Marx, the intellectual Marx, could be the intellectual or even political author... For it was the real—the workers' class struggle—which acted as the true author (the agent)."[14] This is what Marx means when he writes that critical science can only be done by the proletarian class: it is not *Marx* but the class struggle that theorizes and, as such, cannot but do so in a strictly partisan manner. The movement is guided by the educational philosophy of the workers' movement itself, for "the union of theory and practice implies that every political practice contains a philosophy, while every philosophy contains a practical signification, a politics."[15] This is the task of the workers' organization, the Communist Party.

---

13 Ibid., 112.

14 Louis Althusser, *Philosophy of the Encounter*, 18.

15 Louis Althusser, *The Humanist Controversy and Other Writings*, ed. F. Matheron, trans. G.M. Goshgarian (New York: Verso, 2003), 208.

Marx engaged in and performed both pedagogical logics, but in distinct ways at different times, sometimes as an intentional tactic and other times as a contingency of the workers' struggle. In this chapter, I turn to Althusser and Antonio Negri's readings of Marx's writing to excavate his own navigational process, and I do this by focusing on the *Grundrisse* and *Capital* and showing how Marx's own distinction between *inquiry* and *presentation* is not so rigid and, as a result, those who argue in favor of one book over the other do so because they fail to recognize his pedagogical tact. I follow Althusser's notion that "there is no such thing as an innocent reading," and that neither Marx, the interpretations engaged here, nor those that I develop here, are objective or neutral.[16]

My intention in this chapter is not to defend one reading against another or to say one is a 'correct' versus an 'incorrect' interpretation of Marx. I wager that the different presentations are legitimate and productive for the communist struggle. Such a wager, however, is contingent upon an appreciation of Marx's pedagogy, and in particular, his heterogenous blocking together of learning and studying. In other words, the absent pedagogical problematic in both Althusser and Negri underlies the apparent antagonism of their readings. To be faithful to Marx is to learn *and* study works of Marx's and his interpreters—and most importantly the ongoing history of the international struggle of working and oppressed peoples—in order to organize and prepare for a revolution-

---

16 Louis Althusser, "From *Capital* to Marx's Philosophy," in L. Althusser, É. Balibar, R. Establet, P. Macherey, and J. Rancière, *Reading Capital*, trans. B. Brewster and D. Fernbach (New York: Verso, 1965/2015), 12.

ary rupture and build the dictatorship of the proletariat. This does not mean there is the absence of polemical debates but rather that such debates are based on revolutionary optimism. In order to make the strategic shifts and tactical alliances necessary to advance the class struggle, we should maintain the flexibility that constellational thinking allows.

From the *Grundrisse* to *Capital*

Marx's *Grundrisse*, a series of notes Marx wrote in the frantic days of 1857-1858, is seen by some as preparatory research for his magnum opus, *Capital*, especially the first volume, the only one published (and republished) during Marx's lifetime. For Louis Althusser, it is the latter work that constitutes the *one* text by which "Marx has to be *judged*."[17] For others, the notebooks represent a work of Marx in their own right, one that's distinct from and even superior to *Capital*. Antonio Negri, for example, understands the *Grundrisse* as an explicitly *political* text, a *more* marxist text than *Capital* precisely due to its "incredible openness" and its emphasis on antagonistic subjectivity."[18] *Capital*, according to Negri, is not only fragmentary but closed, determinate, and objective, a book where antagonisms are resolved dialectically, foreclosing the subjective rupture that the communist revolution requires. Others insist that we read them together, not necessarily to provide a

17 Louis Althusser, *Lenin and Philosophy and Other Essays*, trans. B. Brewster (New York: Monthly Review Press, 1971), 45.

18 Antonio Negri, *Marx beyond Marx: Lessons on the Grundrisse*, trans. H. Cleaver, M. Ryan, and M. Viano (Brooklyn: Autonomedia, 1979/1991), 9.

final or perfect account of marxism, but rather because such a co-reading generates new insights. Taken together, both present different—but not contradictory—aspects of capital's contemporary forms of exploitation and of proletarian forms of resistance.

Marx's pedagogical gestures here testify to the necessity of both educational praxes. Importantly, however, his movements between learning and studying, while sometimes *tactical* decisions, were not dictated by some inner genius but by the twists and turns of the workers' movement and, undoubtedly, his own health. Marx's serious study of political economy began after the failure of the 1848 bourgeois-democratic revolutions, after which he was exiled to London. He did not see another uprising on the agenda, and so he set to work studying and writing. While he initially introduced his own political and economic categories with *The German Ideology*, his serious study did not begin until much later, in the early 1850s. But when another uprising happened, like the Paris Commune, Marx turned to examine that instead of continuing work on *Capital*. He pushed the publication of volume 2, as he wanted to see how the early 1870s economic crisis turned out.

Marx's notes that were eventually published as the *Grundrisse* were penned during the financial crisis of 1856-7, a crisis that spurred Marx on a frenzy of study. He had a clear goal in mind: to articulate the inner logics and dynamics of capitalism, to critique bourgeois political economy, to lay out a method, and to identify what contradictions could galvanize the revolution. But they were a series of notes, abandoned by Marx and only published first in 1939 in the Soviet Union and made available in Europe and the U.S. during the 1960s and 1970s. As notes, they're traces of studying, and *because* we read Marx studying—that is, producing, following, wondering about, and sometimes losing—concepts as he goes, we can "follow Marx *while he is actually thinking.*"[19]

Negri's 1978 Paris lectures on the *Grundrisse*, delivered at the invitation of Louis Althusser, represent the most partisan approach to the book. It's not that Negri dismisses *Capital*, of course, but that he emphasizes the book only represents one aspect of marxism. The *Grundrisse* is an endless unfolding of antagonisms of revolutionary subjectivity. *Capital*, on the contrary, is more limited precisely because of its "categorical presentation."[20] Pedagogically speaking, the *Grundrisse's* traces of studying open more prospects for revolution that the developmental learning of *Capital* closes down. The difference turns on *antagonism* and *dialectics*. The *Grundrisse* proceeds by way of antagonism, whereas *Capital* proceeds by way of dialectics (which Negri claims are closed and formulaic). Yet the dialectic for Marx is absolutely crucial in both *Capital* and the *Grundrisse*. At the same time, the pedagogical dialectic between learning and studying, for Negri, is incorrectly applied *politically* in *Capital* because of its privileging of presentation and learning, while the *Grundrisse* is a text of studying that includes learning but prioritizes the class struggle, or the pedagogical form of the *Grundrisse* is "open on all sides: every conclusion that takes the form of a presentation of the research opens

---

19 Eric J. Hobsbawm, "Introduction," in K. Marx, *Pre-Capitalist Economic Foundations*, ed. E.J. Hobsbawm, trans. J. Cohen (New York: International Publishers, 1964), 64.

20 Negri, *Marx Beyond Marx*, 8.

spaces to new research and new presentation."[21] The text is one in which "the objective analysis of capital and the subjective analysis of class behavior come together, where class hatred permeates his science."[22] *Capital*, he claims, leaves "no possibility, even in the form of a paradox, of the dynamism of this process by hypostatizing it, by rigidifying it," while "the originality, the happiness, the freshness of the *Grundrisse* rest entirely with its incredible openness."[23] The contradictions of capitalism developed in *Capital* are replaced in the *Grundrisse* with *antagonism* and subjectivity.

The pedagogical *form* of the *Grundrisse*, even the presentation or linearity of the logic, is a *linearity of presentation*, but one determined by "*a class logic that governs this angle of attack of exposition*."[24] The inquiry and presentation of capital are both the antagonism of classes and the differential production of subjectivity. Yet the motor of difference is based on antagonism and the presentation of the theoretical process of inquiry is "a whole series of operations of the *displacement* of the subject and the dislocation of the theoretical field."[25] This is because "class struggle does not know synthesis, it only knows victories and defeats."[26] It's a collective knowledge of wins and

---

21   Ibid., 12.

22   Ibid., 9.

23   Ibid., 61.

24   Ibid.

25   Ibid., 77.

26   Ibid., 76.

losses, advances and retreats, which means that Marx's method opens the path to a theory of surplus-value, which is not
a linear intellectual unfolding of developmental learning but
rather a studying that shifts subjectively and structurally.

Unlike presentation and learning, reality itself "is not linear" but is rather "transformed continually" as it "draws into
its movement the antagonism of collective forces that know-
ingly exercise power," reality and history continually move
the horizon of research. Rather than developmental learning,
it's a studying defined by "a qualitative leap," by "collective
relations of force" and is thus "not skeptical, but dynamic
and creative."[27] As surplus-value is the essence of capital,
this means that capital itself is subjectivity. There is no pre-
determination, no evolution or unraveling; only a process of
studying animated by the indeterminacy and unpredictability
of the class struggle. Through disruption and subversion—in
thought and practice, in the mind and flesh—new *real* categories are born and new antagonisms are animated. Negri
refers to this as a process of *constitution*, one that results from
antagonistic struggles by different and oppositional subjective
forces and that moves from "*the relation between the use value of
abstract knowledge and the need for a transformation of knowledge.*"[28]
Such a transformation is the *production of reality*.

In sum, for Negri what is important in the *Grundrisse* is
not so much the formulation of new categories and concepts,

---

27 Ibid., 56.

28 Ibid., 47.

but rather "the definition of *social antagonism*."[29] The pedagogy
that dominates the *Grundrisse*, in this reading, is one of re-
lentless studying organized around and for communism. Yet
it *advances*, *retreats*, and *suspends* the developmental learning at
work in the book. In fact, the two pedagogies are constellated
together. Marx does not finalize one aspect of research and
move to the next logical one. Instead, each inquiry uncovers
a distinct antagonistic subjectivity and struggle, which renews
and compels the formulation of categories and concepts,
until the next antagonism displaces the field of studying and
learning altogether. Learning here is subordinated to studying
insofar as the presentation itself structures and produces antagonism. Whereas the knowledge presented in *Capital* is fixed
and rigid, for Negri, the knowledge of the *Grundrisse* is open
and indeterminate.

The Pedagogies of *Capital*

While Althusser finds that the texts later compiled as the *Economic and Philosophical Manuscripts of 1844* were totally idealist, he still sees the transitional works "like *The German Ideology*, or even the *Grundrisse*" as "*very ambiguous*," *too Hegelian*
and thus not *marxist* in their theory, science, philosophy, or
praxis.[30] The epistemological break or rupture he justifies in
For Marx happens as clarity overtakes ambiguity. The break is
two-fold: it entails "founding the theory of history (historical
materialism)" as well as producing "a new philosophy (dialectical materialism)" that happened when he "broke with his

---

29 Ibid., 187.

30 Althusser, *Lenin and Philosophy and Other Essays*, 45.

erstwhile ideological philosophy."[31] In his later work "Marx in his Limits" Althusser says the labeling was imprudent but it still rings true. It does so not because of Marx's intellect but as a result of Marx's participation in the organizations and parties of the class, especially the First International, in that these themselves produced the rupture he would later write as *Capital*.[32] Earlier, Althusser conceived it as a break that *Marx himself produced* that emphasizes clarity.

In his contribution to *Reading Capital*, Althusser focuses on the scientific nature of *Capital*, and how its new epistemology and framework changes the world (and the word). Althusser articulates, in content and form, the pedagogical and political modes of engaging *Capital*. He presents this through two forms of reading-writing. He begins by noting that the book is a series of lecture notes from a class in 1965, which have not been edited to create (the illusion of?) a *completed* work, and instead remain "the mere beginnings of a *reading*," which therefore retain "their rhythm, their didactic or oral style, but also and above all in their discrepancies, the repetitions, hesitations and uncertain steps in their investigations."[33] By doing so, "all the risks and advantages of this adventure are reproduced; so that the reader will be able to find in them new-born the experience of a reading; and so that he in turn will be dragged in the wake of this first reading into a second one which will take

---

31 Louis Althusser, *For Marx*, trans. B. Brewster (New York: Verso, 1965/2005), 33.

32 Althusser, *Philosophy of the Encounter*, 31.

33 Althusser, "From *Capital* to Marx's Philosophy," 11.

us still further."[34] Both kinds of reading-writing and speaking-listening practices block learning and studying together, but the stated goal is *clarity* for both.

The first practice, however, is *not marxist*, and occurs when "Marx reads his predecessor's discourse (Smith's for instance) through his own discourse. The result of this reading through a grid… is merely a summary of concordances and discordances, the balances of what Smith discovered and what he missed."[35] This is a reading in which "the logic of a conception of knowledge in which all the work of knowledge is reduced in principle to the recognition of the mere relation of *vision*; in which the whole nature of its object is reduced to the mere condition of a *given*."[36] To remain here is to remain trapped in "the mirror myth of knowledge as the vision of a given object or the reading of an established text, neither of which is ever anything but transparency itself."[37] The truth of an object is *within* the object and is obtained by abstracting the truth from the object, just like "gold is *extracted* (or abstracted, i.e., separated) from the dross of earth and sand in which it is held and contained."[38] Here, knowledge's "sole function is to separate, in the object, the two parts which exist in it, the essential and the inessential—by special procedures whose

34 Ibid., 12.

35 Ibid., 16.

36 Ibid., 17.

37 Ibid.

38 Ibid., 35.

aim is to *eliminate the inessential real...* and to leave the knowing subject only the second part of the real which is its essence, itself real."[39] The essence is hidden, invisible, and we *discover* or *grasp* it in the "most literal sense: removing the covering, as the husk is removed from the nut."[40]

The second reading, which we could call a marxist reading, focuses not on sights and oversights, but the connections or flows between the visible and invisible, and concerns the possibility of sight itself, in which "non-vision is therefore inside vision, it is a form of vision and hence has a necessary relationship with vision."[41] Hence, we can discover a new conception of knowledge, as against immediate and essential reading, in which the text mirrors knowledge. Instead, we have knowledge and the production of knowledge, the movement of knowledge produced through the *flesh* of collective subjectivities in struggle. What does the invisible within the visible mean? That writing and reading "can only pose problems on the terrain and within the horizon of a definite theoretical structure, its problematic, which constitutes its absolute and definite conditions of possibility, and hence the absolute determination of *the forms in which all problems must be posed*, at a given moment in the science."[42] This reading is one in which the eye does not *see* the field, but *sees itself seeing*, or listens to its listening! "It is literally no longer the eye (the mind's eye)

---

39 Ibid., 36.

40 Ibid., 37.

41 Ibid., 19.

42 Ibid., 23, emphasis in original.

of a subject which *sees* what exists in the field defined by a theoretical problematic: it is this field itself which *sees itself* in the objects or problems it defines."[43] The invisible is not the *outside* of the visible, which would only necessitate an immediate reading of the unread. Instead, "the invisible is defined by the visible as *its* invisible, *its* forbidden vision: the invisible is not therefore simply what is outside the visible," "the outer darkness of exclusion—but the *inner darkness of exclusion*, inside the visible itself because defined by its structure."[44] The limits to the text are *internal* to it; they represent the traces of study and invite us back to inquiry with its meandering messiness and unpredictable lineages.

This marxist reading does not come from "the idealist myth of a mental decision to change 'viewpoints,'" but instead involves a "real transformation of the means of production of knowledge."[45] Knowledge is something *active* that's produced *through writing and reading*. "Perhaps," Althusser proffers, "it is not impermissible to think that if Marx does 'play' so much with Hegelian formulae in certain passages, the game is not just raffishness or sarcasm, but *the action of a real drama*, in which old concepts desperately play the part of something absent *which is nameless*, in order to call it onto the stage in person."[46] Drama is a scientific staging of the invisible within the visible that "only progresses, i.e., lives, by the extreme at-

---

43 Ibid., 24.

44 Ibid., 25.

45 Ibid., 26.

46 Ibid., 28.

tention it pays to the points where it is theoretically fragile."[47]
Science is not about uncovering something that was previously covered, but about listening to silences in the content and
the form, perhaps by listening to the *nuance* or *timbre* of the
matter of writing, which is thought in action—as opposed to
knowledge in stasis.

This approach to reading-writing is philosophical and
scientific for Althusser, which means that it questions the relation of the text to its object while questioning the object itself. This entails changing our understandings of fundamental
processes, "the 'simplest' acts of existence: seeing, listening,
speaking, reading" and revising them against both religious
and empiricist readings, summed up as *essentialist* or *immediate*
readings.[48] Immediate or empiricist reading-writing is that of
the young Marx, who believed that in order to "know the essence of things" one had "simply to *read*… in black and white
the presence of the 'abstract' essence in the transparency of
its 'concrete' existence."[49] It was not necessary to account for
the structure in which the text is situated and with which it
does its *work*. Althusser absently tells us that in *Capital*, Marx's
inquiry-study and presentation-learning are again constellated.
Marx, he reminds us, is above all "a *reader* who *reads* to us; and
out loud;" Marx "felt the need to fill out his text by reading
out loud, not only for the pleasure of quotation, or through
scrupulousness in his references" because of both "the intel-

---

47 Ibid., 29.

48 Ibid., 13.

49 Ibid., 14.

lectual honesty which made him always generously recognize his debts" and "the theoretical conditions of his work of discovery."[50] This is a doubled reading, with each form operating on different pedagogical logics.

The question is whether each reading produces a more accurate form of knowledge or whether it always entails rendering an opacity transparent. In fact, it does *both*. We produce knowledge, but there is *always a dislocation* between the *real object* and the *object of knowledge*. Against Hegel, Marx insisted that "the concrete in thought" remain "distinct from its presupposition, the real subject, society."[51] Knowledge is circular, in that it produces something that was already there, but we do not merely *turn around* in the circle "because this circle is not the closed circle of ideology, but the circle perpetually opened by its closures themselves."[52] As Lucia Pradella writes, such a separation makes central "the nexus between theory and praxis" because "only by acting within this movement could the theoretical critique conceive of capitalist society as a contradictory and transitory system."[53] Althusser's interpretation of Marx's theory of *Capital* is anti-Hegelian not only because it's open beyond ideology but because its distinguishing feature

---

50 Ibid., 16.

51 Lucia Pradella, *Globalisation and the Critique of Political Economy: New Insights from Marx's Writings* (New York: Routledge, 2016), 132.

52 Althusser, "From *Capital* to Marx's Philosophy," 72.

53 Pradella, *Globalisation and the Critique of Political Economy*, 132.

"is that it fights for openness."[54] One *pedagogical* way Althusser's writing does this, David Backer shows, is by employing "scare quotes," which indicates that "the word has competing concepts. The person who writes the word is not innocent, nor the person reading it. They work with a problematic that arises out of their moment, experience, and their material situation."[55] They are indications of ongoing study, of irresoluteness, of the openness of antagonistic materialism and the communist struggle.

The Open Inconclusiveness of *Capital*

Negri's critique of *Capital* is not total in any way. But he insists that the later work's method of presentation—the pedagogy of learning with its developmental logics and seemingly progressive conceptual creations—overtakes and subsumes the method of inquiry—the pedagogy of studying that responds, revives, and displaces such concepts through antagonistic differences within the totality of capital. The class struggle over the working day is replaced by the organic composition of capital, and the struggle is not defined by exploitation but "on private and competitive capital" rather than "*social capital*."[56] *Capital*'s categories are "objectified," which "blocks action by revolutionary subjectivity."[57] Even if *Capital* is organized more

---

54 David I. Backer, *The Gold and the Dross: Althusser for Educators* (Boston: Brill, 2019), 52.

55 Ibid., 36.

56 Negri, *Marx beyond Marx*, 27.

57 Ibid., 8.

along the lines of learning, on my reading, there are still traces of antagonistic subjectivity, of differential manifestations
of struggle, and the interruption of studying in presentation.
There are traces of studying throughout.

One example is the very last chapter of the first volume
of *Capital*, which is concerned with Wakefield's theory of colonialism. It's a rather dry and short chapter, one that follows
from Marx's most succinct case and call for communist revolution, where Marx turns away from the historical empirical
inquiry and presents a succinct dialectical and historical mate-
rialist analysis of the tendency of capitalist accumulation and
how the contradictions of capitalism might result in particular
revolutionary paths. Marx begins with the scattered private
property of individuals in petty manufacture, handicraft, and
peasant labor. Together, these prevent the concentration of
means of production, division of labor, and cooperation of
labor (social labor), the formation of the collective laborer
(the antagonistic subject), and so remains locked within the
production and circulation of use-values.

Halfway through this first paragraph of the second to last
chapter, Marx notes that "at a certain stage of development,"
these property relations create "the material agencies for its
own dissolution," producing "new passions" that "the old
social organization" prevents.[58] Individual private property is
annihilated by capital and, through theft, colonialism, slavery,
repression, and so on, centralized and concentrated by capital. At the same time, this produces the collective laborer and
a social process of work that develops a universal (although

---

58 *Capital (Vol. 1)*, 714.

not undifferentiated) social worker. As capital concentrates the means of production and the proletarian class, the latter's rebellious nature grows. Capital is now a fetter on production:

> The monopoly of capital becomes a fetter upon the mode of production, which has sprung up and flourished along with and under it. centralization of the means of production and socialization of labor at last reach a point where they become incompatible with their capitalist integument. This integument is burst asunder. The knell of capitalist private property sounds. The expropriators are expropriated.[59]

He ends with a speculation on the relative violence of both revolutionary processes. Whereas the centralization and concentration of capital were "incomparably more protracted, violent, and difficult than the transformation of capitalistic private property… into socialized property."[60] The former entailed the dispossession, theft, and exploitation of the many by the few, while the latter might entail the expropriation of the few by the many. That's how he ends this brief penultimate chapter. Yet it's not an empirical contradiction but an articulation of contradictions. There's nothing indicating a mechanical or deterministic prediction.

Why not end here? One answer is that Marx is engaging with Hegel. David Harvey first introduced this claim in *The Limits to Capital*. Harvey's view is that the chapter is ultimately

---

59 Ibid., 715.

60 Ibid.

a Hegelian formulation that proposes "colonial solutions" to demonstrate that "the conditions that gave rise to the problems in the first place are simply replicated anew."[61] As a result, the question of geographic expansion and the production of space remain "unresolved in Marxian theory."[62] While there are indeed important debates over imperialism and its relationship to the internal contradictions of capital, missed in Harvey's answer is the pedagogical form of *Capital*. The ending of volume 1 ultimately returns us to studying and to the antagonistic class forces that animate marxist theory and practice. The dialectic in chapter 32 may seem teleological and closed, but the brief exposition in chapter 33 undoes that. There are no guarantees, no objective determinants divorced from subjective differences or the class struggle. Marx returns us to study and to struggle, as I hope this book's presentation does.

---

61 David Harvey, *The Limits to Capital* (New York: Verso, 1982/2007), 414.

62 Ibid., 415.

2

ANTI-COLONIAL ENCOUNTERING THROUGH ERRANT LEARNING

In *Learning to Divide the World*, John Willinsky examines the role of educational projects in colonialism. The educational dynamic here unfolds in three steps: discovery and possession, exhibition, and the colonial school. Together these three steps work to produce a certain "planetary consciousness" that included "a distinctly educational fascination with the world."[1] While Willinsky introduces the notion that learning might have a connection to colonialism, he never takes this up through a questioning of what learning is as a distinct educational philosophy. Accordingly, his responses resort to content changes in curriculum, like supplements for different subject areas that would address their colonial legacies. At the same time, educational philosophers who continue to demonstrate the myriad problems with the dominance of learning

---

1 John Willinsky, *Learning to Divide the World: Education at Empire's End* (Minneapolis: University of Minnesota Press, 1998), 40.

have located their critiques within problems of capitalism or neoliberalism, demonstrating how learning—which has itself become a kind of economic transaction—tethers individualized subjects to the shifting needs of global capital. The *global* of capital remains implicit in this research. There is, as such, a pressing need for educational philosophy to investigate the relationship between pedagogical logics, colonization, and decolonization.

Through an educational reading of Édouard Glissant's *Poetics of Space* and Peter Sloterdijk's *Spheres* project, this chapter draws out and develops two related aerial educational philosophies (grasping and lordly imagining) that propel colonization. Expanding these same texts, it begins developing a theory of errant learning as an alternative educational philosophy with anticolonial and decolonial potentiality. Specifically, with Glissant's minor remarks on different forms of conceptualizing understanding, I identify the grasping drive as the educational foundation of the colonizing apparatus. I argue that the grasping drive positions opacity as a potential that *must* be realized—as a thought that *must* be known—an orientation that ends up sacrificing opacity as such. After articulating the other form of understanding he offers—giving-on-and-with—which turns away from enclosures and opens into Relation, I point to a potential contradiction in this division as it relates to his overall project: namely, that enclosures are necessary for the struggle against colonialism. By freeing grasping from the grasping drive, I reposition the relationship between grasping and giving-on-and-with in a way that allows for certain kinds of enclosures.

The relationship between openness and enclosure introduces the question of pedagogical *form*, and it's at this point that I turn to Sloterdijk's sphereological investigations. Reading the colonizing phase of globalization through Sloterdijk's notion of lordly imagining—which I link to the grasping drive—I then draw out how different educational processes produce different kinds of spheres, ones with colonizing and decolonizing potential. Finally, I articulate errant learning as a process of grasping and giving-on-with that values the air over the ground and opacity *qua* opacity to produce foam formations with attention to the history of inequality and injury through immune deprivation. Errant learning is another form of dialectically blocking together the methods of inquiry and presentation, but one that shows the necessity of presentation and the existing historical material conditions in which we engage in inquiry.

An Opening: The Grasping Drive

An expansive thinker who traversed a variety of disciplines and forms, one major focus of Glissant's work is decolonization. Scholars tend to divide his work down the line of his 1980 Ph.D. thesis. Celia Britton contends that his early works were properly anticolonial and focused primarily on Martinique, while the later works were more postcolonial and focused on the world through the lens of the Caribbean.[2] Nick Nesbitt has a less sympathetic take, conceptualizing the turn from "anticolonial political struggle to an autonomy of cultural production," which he claims Glissant realized in *Poetics*

---

2 Celia Britton, "Globalization and Political Action in the Work of Édouard Glissant," *Small Axe* 13, no. 3 (2009): 1-11.

of Relation.[3] While I'm more inclined to agree with Britton, and I do want to draw out how his anticolonial commitments show up in *Poetics of Relation*, an analysis of Glissant's *oeuvre* is outside the scope of this chapter. I choose to follow H. Aldai Murdoch's advice, that "defining or categorizing Glissant could be said to be a function of which aspect of his work one wants to emphasize."[4] Such an approach, as we will see, is potentially more in line with Glissant's idea of Relation, which resists any totalizing captures.

In this section, I introduce Glissant's rather quick division of understanding into two antagonistic features, which provide the beginnings of a theory of errant learning. To do this, however, it's helpful to have some context about the overall project in which they appear.

Glissant's *Poetics of Relation* is a series of gestures that work collectively to reconfigure the world from system to chaos, from rootedness to errantry, from filiation to expanse, from colonization to decolonization. At a few different moments in the texts, he offers what I take up as fragments of an educational philosophy that can help us to both understand the educational dynamics of colonization and imagine an anticolonial or decolonial educational dynamic: grasping (*comprehendre*) and

---

3 Nick Nesbitt, "Early Glissant: From the Destitution of the Political to Antillean Ultra-Leftism," *Callaloo* 36, no. 4 (2013): 937.

4 H. Aldai Murdoch, "Édouard Glissant's Creolized World Vision: From Resistance to Relation to *Opacité*," *Callaloo* 36, no. 4 (2013): 876.

giving-on-and-with (*donner-avec*).[5] Both of these take up and deploy a certain relationship to what Glissant refers to as Relation, the broader concept he cobbles together in the book.

Relation begins with the slave trade and the figure of the "open boat." Glissant begins with the slave ship, that container of unspeakable suffering, that terrorist vessel trafficking in human bodies. He asks us to imagine the magnitude and particularities of the torture, corruption, and depravity the slave ship contains even as they are, as he insists throughout the book, literally unimaginable. The international slave trade is a triple abyss of the cargo hold, the seas, and the separation of culture and tradition. Yet this abyss is not vacuous. It instead is a breeding ground of Relation: "The populations that then formed, despite having forgotten the chasm, despite being unable to imagine the passion of those who foundered there, nonetheless wove this sail (a veil). They did not use it to return to the Former Land but rose up on this unexpected, dumbfounded land."[6] This is where we get our first glimpse of Glissant's open dialectical sensitivity, as evidenced by the excessive surplus of the regime of slavery, with its subordination and resistance.[7] The abyss of the slave-trade is both a capture and a clearing. We also approach his educational project, as the

---

5 "Grasping" and "giving-on-and-with" are Betsy Wing's translations (see Wing, 1997, p. xiv).

6 Édouard Glissant, *Poetics of Relation*, trans. B. Wing (Ann Arbor: The University of Michigan Press, 1997), 7-8.

7 For more on his reworking or "bypassing" of Hegelian dialectics, see Alexandre Leupin, "The Slave's *Jouissance*," *Callaloo* 36, no. 4 (2013): 890-901.

abyss metamorphoses into "knowledge of Relation within the Whole," which is not a set of concrete information but an orientation toward the world. Slave ships are now open boats, "and we sail them for everyone."[8]

The origins of the open boat are not relegated to memory or irrelevance, which is why openness is not exactly like the rhizomatic nomadism of Deleuze and Guattari. Rhizomatic nomadism is a helpful concept in that it gets us thinking in terms of relations and extension, but it needs to be historicized because the nomad's "freedom" is "a form of obedience to contingencies that are restrictive."[9] At the same time as the open boat contains its origins, it's not determined or explained solely by them. To navigate in Relation's waters, the open boat needs an expansive errantry rather than a restrictive filiation, to look outward and beyond rather than only down. Colonialism, as he sees it, is in part the movement, production, and deepening of roots that ground identity. This is implicit "at first ('my root is the strongest') and then is explicitly exported as value ('a person's worth is determined by his root')."[10]

This colonial framework still exerts its dominance, as evidenced by the struggle for recognition by claiming similarity or difference from the colonizer. "Decolonization," as he sees it, "will have done its real work when it goes beyond this limit."[11] Crucially, this too is a historical process conditioned

---

8 Glissant, *Poetics of Relation*, 8, 9.

9 Ibid., 12.

10 Ibid., 17.

11 Ibid.

by contingency, rather than a call to forget the nation or to reject borders. The struggle for Relation entails the movement toward *inter*dependence, "but the absolute presupposition of this interdependence is that instances of independence will be defined as closely as possible and actually won or sustained."[12] Despite the decisive phrasing, the "absolute presupposition" of genuine independence is not a temporal prerequisite to interdependence, a prior state that must be achieved and then negated through sublation into another state. Instead, the struggle *against* colonialism occurs contemporaneously with the struggle *beyond* colonialism. Pursued separately, the former allows history to determine the boat's existence while the latter idealistically feigns to forget history. To sail beyond the limit of colonialism requires both strategies.

Aside from tying the colonized identity to the roots of the colonizer through opposition, which remains under the umbrella of colonialism, filiation hinders Relation in another crucial and broader way. Filiation traces meaning and identity back through roots, which for Glissant rests on the notion that these can be known and made fully transparent. The roots and the identity and meaning derived therefrom are never fully known or revealed, but any and all uncertainty or ignorance about them are, at least as a matter of principle, structural properties that the subject can overcome. Opacity is here positioned as an obstacle to transparency. The epistemological mission of colonialism is precisely to overcome this obstacle: "If we examine the process of 'understanding' people and ideas from the perspective of Western thought, we

---

12 Ibid., 143.

discover that its basis is this requirement for transparency."[13] This is even the case for those who advocate for the accommodations of difference in a global village, as those who do the accommodating place the other within the existing system.

The ontology of transparency frames the world as graspable, as capable of being brought into one's own knowledge and understanding. Grasping is only explicitly mentioned five times in the book (one of which takes on a positive form in Relation). Grasping is only defined towards the end: "the verb *to grasp* contains the movement of hands that grab their surroundings and bring them back to themselves. A gesture of enclosure if not appropriation."[14] On my reading, grasping is the pedagogical drive of colonialism, positioning the subject as one who has not only the *right* but the *requirement* to reach out and bring the world into themselves. The opacity of the world—its land, water, and inhabitants—exists only for the learner to grab it, make it transparent, and incorporate it into their understanding. The grasping drive is the educational foundation of the colonial apparatus that wages a war on opacity by positioning it as a potential that *must* be realized so it can be held onto.

Beyond Grasping and into Relation

Glissant shows us how the grasping drive itself organizes being, knowing, and relating through a colonial framework. To get at his other conceptualization of understanding, that of giving-on-and-with, it's necessary to dive into the unfolding

---

13 Ibid., 189-190.

14 Ibid., 191-192.

of Relation, which the colonial grasping drive blocks. First, one can only gesture towards this Relation. In the book, Glissant gathers together fragments of openings in a poetics that cannot systematize but "is latent, open, multilingual in intention, directly in contact with everything possible."[15] Second, the site through which he approaches Relation is the Caribbean, as it's one place with particularly dense relations, as evidenced by one relational process that begins to approach Relation: creolization. Creolization is a process of hybridization that "is only exemplified by its processes and certainly not by the 'contents' on which these operate."[16] Glissant places the page of the book bearing the heading of "Creolizations" at the beginning of the section titled "Paths," because creolization is a pathway into relation, not a mere representation or consolidation of it. Nonetheless, the pathway is one that's contingently determined through actual historical processes, ones of enclosure and expanse.

Any attempt to represent Relation would necessarily reduce it, fixing it in time and place and ultimately *denying* Relation. Because Relation is an ever-shifting totality, it cannot be totalized. To clarify this, Glissant introduces the concept of *chaos-monde*. *Chaos-monde* is not a chaotic world, but a world full of energy. It has norms, but they come neither before nor after what takes place, neither *a priori* nor *a posteriori*; it's "neither fusion nor confusion: it acknowledges neither the uniform

---

15 Ibid., 32.

16 Ibid., 89.

blend… nor muddled nothingness."[17] When everything is relational, each movement transforms the totality of *chaos-monde*, and as long as movement takes place the totality transforms.

Relation is a realm of challenge, exhaustion, and reinvention. The open boat offers an alternative way of encountering the world and the self as it sails the waters of the *chaos-monde*. Whereas the colonizing ships sail the waters of a world that can be grasped, cataloged, explicated, and frozen into artifacts, the open boats enter into a Relation that's impossible to fasten or contain. That the totality of Relation is ungraspable and unknowable does not mean that it's useless or colonizing to present knowledge about it, only that this knowledge will necessarily be *in* and not *of* Relation. Grasping is, to be sure, only one way to approach understanding, one that gives it "a fearsome repressive meaning."[18]

Against grasping, Glissant offers a form of understanding as "the gesture of giving-on-and-with that opens finally on totality."[19] Under this heading, understanding is not an act of taking something external and incorporating it into the subject, but becomes instead a generation that emerges from Relation that the subject contributes back to Relation. Because the subject exists in Relation and is composed of relations, the subject and Relation change through giving-on-and-with through which we encounter the force of disinterpellation and are subject to the structural swerves of the world.

---

17 Ibid., 94.

18 Ibid., 26.

19 Ibid., 192.

Giving-on-and-with entails a radically different pedagogical orientation than grasping, a difference that I believe hinges on the association between transparency and opacity. Insofar as grasping positions the world as transparent, giving-on-and-with positions the world as opaque and transparency as impossibility. Indeed, if Relation is a constantly transforming totality that morphs with each movement, any attempt to render even one part of Relation transparent would not only be partial, but would itself again change Relation. Glissant shows this dynamism with a few words about what a language of Relation would look like:

> One can imagine language diasporas that would change so rapidly within themselves and with such feedback, so many turnarounds of norms… that their fixity would lie in that change. Their ability to endure would not be accessible through deepening but through the shimmer of variety. It would be a fluid equilibrium. This linguistic sparkle, so far removed from the mechanics of sabirs and codes, is still inconceivable for us, but only because we are paralyzed to this day by monolingual prejudice ('my language is my root').[20]

Relation is opaque through and through because it cannot be divided into its aliquot parts at any moment in time. There are no prime or elemental components of Relation because each and every element is itself the product of the relations that comprise Relation; the particularities of Rela-

---

20 Ibid., 98.

tion are, in other words, cut across by internal and external relations that are always changing. This does not mean that giving-on-and-with eschews knowledge or condemns transparency. Nor does it mean that we should throw up our hands and *give up* understanding altogether. On the contrary, in Relational understanding, the desire to know is driven by the impossibility of fully knowing some foundational truths. Even Relation and its opacity are not demonstrable truths. "Relation," Glissant writes, "cannot be 'proved,' because its totality is not approachable. But it can be imagined, conceivable in transport of thought."[21] Totality is never fixed and so cannot be grasped, but we nonetheless can aim for it. We aim for it, knowing beforehand our inevitable failure, aware of the inescapable opacity of Relation. Always partial, temporary, uncertain, and unsure of itself, knowledge is a kind of imagining, something that might and might not be. It's an endless immersion in the dialectic of inquiry and presentation.

Murdoch puts the connection between opacity and decolonization succinctly: "The notion that one can recognize otherness, and be complicit with it in a positive way instead of attempting to challenge, appropriate, erase, or assimilate it, is an idea that breaks with longstanding universalist and imperial practices."[22] As such, for Glissant decolonization must entail the "right to opacity," which is distinct from the right to difference. The right to difference is progressive relative to the denial of difference, but it remains trapped within the pedagogy of grasping. We have to push beyond the right to

21 Ibid., 174.

22 Murdoch, "Édouard Glissant's Creolized World Vision," 887.

difference and "agree also to the right to opacity that is not enclosure within an impenetrable autarchy but subsistence within an irreducible singularity."[23] Note that Glissant is not against the right to difference but insists that this right is *also* recognized with the right to opacity. Just as interdependence is tied up with independence, so too is opacity tied up with difference. Thus, it's important that we also historicize the right to opacity rather than uncritically celebrate it.[24] If we rearrange difference such that it's necessarily opaque, then each act of national independence is the creation of a new relay in Relation rather than the re-establishment of a former pure origin. Newly independent nations collect, produce, and disperse new relations. Or, as Glissant formulates it, "every (self-)determination" is "a generative distancing."[25] The pursuit of independence and interdependence would occur simultaneously as the colonized identity is mobilized to assert its right to difference *and* opacity.

The Glissant of *Poetics of Relation* is sensitive to the history and power that's brought us to Relation via colonization and creolization—by oppression and resistance. From this imperative, he theorizes different (and seemingly antagonistic) processes concurrently. Yet this is not quite maintained with his division of understanding into grasping and giving-on-and-with. While grasping encloses Relation, at one point

---

23 Glissant, *Poetics of Relation*, 190.

24 For more on this, see Derek R. Ford and Tyson E. Lewis, "On the Freedom to be Opaque Monsters: Communist Pedagogy, Aesthetics, and the Sublime," *Cultural Politics* 14, no. 1 (2018): 95-108.

25 Glissant, *Poetics of Relation*, 153.

in the book he notes that imagination "helps us to grasp the (not prime) elements of our totality."[26] Grasping is not after the base or raw materials of totality, as it proceeds with a conception of an indivisible Relation. This particular appearance of grasping in the book is, I hold, one that has been liberated from the grasping *drive*. Grasping itself is still an act of reaching out and bringing in, and so it's still an act of enclosure, but because of its orientation to opacity, the enclosure is not ever complete. We might visualize the grasping drive as reaching out, grabbing with the hand, closing the hand, and returning the hand to the subject, whereas grasping freed from the grasping drive would reach out, grab with the hand open, bending the fingers toward the palm but keeping them separated, and returning to the subject. Grasping, as a practice of errant learning, is an act of partial and temporary enclosure, one that would still allow the subject to give-on-and-with Relation at the same time as they focus on their enclosures and protections; a relationship that's consistent with the simultaneity of independence and interdependence, self-determination and interrelation. In this way, errant learning exists in Relation but facilitates certain forms of enclosures within Relation. As a result, the question of *form* is key for errant learning.

Educational Forms of Inquiry and Presentation

Being is necessarily a being-*in*, and the question of what it is that we're *in* is one that, according to Sloterdijk, philosophy has not explicitly considered. His answer, which takes the form of a speculative grand narrative of history and philos-

26 Ibid., 170.

ophy, is that humans are always in spheres, which are protective immune systems that are constantly created and recreated. Spheres are both actual and metaphorical containers, material and conceptual, both literal spaces like wombs and houses, classrooms and cities, and figurative ones like families and collectives, subcultures, and clubs. As he shows in his three books—*Bubbles, Globes,* and *Foams*—different spheres have different histories, ambitions, dispositions, capacities, politics, and, as I argue, pedagogies, that can help us think more clearly about the educational form of errant learning and distinguish between different acts of enclosure. In turn, fleshing out errant learning adds a new pedagogical conceptualization of spherical formations, highlighting how they are always necessarily educational projects of inquiry and presentation.

Bubbles serve as immunological containers for humans. They're literal-figural encasings we work again and again to create and recreate to provide a protective film between an outside and us. As elemental forms of being-in, bubbles seek to expand. A new educational philosophy is birthed: lordly imagining, a grasping that takes the spherical form of an enclosure, as the microsphere expands into the macrosphere. This growth process is one in which the microsphere brings that which is outside into the interior through incorporation, inclusion, and neutralization.[27] Extension augments the immunological qualities and capacities of the sphere, protecting the inside while prospectively looking to the outside. The

---

27 It's worth (foot)noting that for Sloterdijk this lordly imagining and the resulting spheric expansion only developed in full in China, India, and Greece,

growth of cities is an example of spheric expansion that highlights the role of lordly imagining in globalization. The development of walled-in cities demonstrates this principle: "the outside world increasingly ceased to be an ungovernable environment, opening up more and more as the private world of the first lords who touched, explored, described and comprehended it."[28] Importantly, as cities grow so too does the thickness of their walls. Along these lines, the transition from microsphere to macrosphere is one driven forward by the drive to detail, catalog, and ultimately own the outside, and in this way works against the unfolding of Relation.

If we appreciate the role of lordly imagining in macrospheric extension, we can understand the shift from celestial to terrestrial globalization as the logical outcome of the grasping drive. The pursuit of measuring the immeasurable led to the discovery that the earth itself is a star and that, like all stars, it has a finite life expectancy. Aesthetically speaking, the sublime of the heavens gave way to the beauty of the earth. Or, as Sloterdijk presents it, "terrestrial globalization was the victory of the interesting over the ideal. Its result, the earth made known, was the unsmooth orb, which disappoints as a form but attracts attention as an interesting body."[29] Terrestrial globalization was the grasping drive internalized from the dyadic orbs to the one earth orb. "Discovery" itself becomes synonymous with grasping, as it "denotes the epitome of practices whereby the unknown is transformed into

---

28 Peter Sloterdijk, *Spheres II: Globes: Macrosphereology*, trans. W. Hoban (Los Angeles: Semiotext(e), 1999/2014), 290.

29 Ibid., 772.

the known, the unimagined into the imagined. With regard
to the still largely unexplored, undepicted, undescribed and
unexploited earth, this means that procedures and media had
to be found to bring these into the picture as a whole and in
detail."[30]

Before terrestrial globalization, discovery named the process of taking the cover off an object. Under this definition,
discovery is "an exposure of the known;" after colonialism,
it denotes "the finding of something unknown."[31] In educational terms, colonialism is a war on opacity in the name of a
final transparency; in pedagogical terms, it's a war on research
in the name of a final presentation. Such a move would be
decidedly anti-communist, if we recall Marx and Engels' definition of communism from *The German Ideology* as "the *real*
movement which abolishes the present state."[32]

This final transparency undergirds the movement of capital across the globe. Only if something is known and delin-
eated can it be owned and transferred. Rendering something
transparent enables one to secure a return on investment.
Maps, as records of discoveries, were means of acquiring and
transferring land and its inhabitants (That the "new" lands
conquered often had prefixes of "new" or "south" attached
to them is a telling linguistic connection between colonialism
and filiation): "Europeans enjoyed the prerogative of seman-
tically cloning their world and appropriating the distant and

---

30 Ibid., 862.

31 Ibid., 868.

32 Marx and Engels, *The German Ideology*, 56-57.

foreign points through the lexical recurrence of the same."[33] Despite its pretenses and self-assurances of objectivity, the lordly imagination cannot get outside of itself. Cartography and geography are object lessons through which we can get a sense of the operations and outcomes of the lordly imagination's macrospherical expansion. Artists and writers communicated the newly discovered knowledges in ways that had more popular appeal than maps and land deeds, rounding off the edges of more specialized discourses.

While Europeans thought they were bringing the world inside of their monosphere, something quite different was happening. Instead of deepening their roots and centrality, they were engaged in expanse and decentralization. This is what accounts for the fact that the Western mass media has only recently been struck by the need to consider globalization, this process that's been underway since the first cosmologists looked to the sky. Now that globalization is over, the West is finally forced to come to grips with the fact that the socialist, national liberation, and other anti-imperialist and decolonizing struggles of varying sizes collectively popped so many holes in the macrosphere. Terrestrial globalization was "a spatial revolution into the outside" that transformed places into locations on maps through an equivocation of different distances and a symmetricalization of space; the dominant colonizing cities and states lost their centrality and claims to rootedness. [34] Decolonization teaches the colonizing world the lesson of terrestrial globalization as the open boat sails on the

33 Sloterdijk, *Spheres II*, 886.

34 Ibid., 791.

seas, on which traffic now runs (at least) two ways.

Errant Learning in Foams

If celestial globalization ends with the dethroning of the ideal by the interesting, then terrestrial globalization ends with the exhaustion of the outside. The fully circumnavigated globe takes on a new form that "is produced simultaneity, and it finds its convergence in things that are current"[35] Foams are the remnants of imploded projects of producing the singular Earth macrospheric bubble, formations that contain multiple simultaneous bubbles.

After the efforts to produce a solid and fixed macrospheric container for humanity fail, after the impossibility—and with that, hopefully, the disagreeability—of the search for a final monosphere is revealed, we see the need to reconceptualize our sphereological imperative reality with the form of something lighter, more flexible, and less permanent. Orienting ourselves in this direction, however, will remain impossible without an alternative pedagogical form. In this final section, I draw together the educational-political observations produced through the chapter to suggest how errant learning produces foam formations. This, in turn, allows us to understand the dynamic relations between grasping and giving-on-and-with of errant learning, or the dialectical navigation between presentation and inquiry.

If we picture ourselves on the stern of Glissant's open boat as we sail the waters of the *chaos-monde*, we can see the foam forming white caps on the waves of our wake. The slave

---

35 Ibid., 939.

ships of colonialism in their search for the rationalization and domination of the Earth through the construction of the one orb, cannot help but produce a new spatial morphology. The foam is a collective of co-mingling bubbles, as liquid film envelopes air (which in turn makes bubbles light, allowing them to rise to the surface). If we keep on looking, we'll see the foam's ephemerality, as the film thins and pops, and the air escapes. Foam has "no life expectancy of next generation, all it knows is running ahead into its own bursting."[36] Ignorant of all filiation, foam bubbles do not set down any roots, rejecting fundamental and stable ground in favor of pneumatic expanse (and collapse). Relation takes the form of foams, "where the dreamers and agitators are at home; one will never find the adults, the serious and those with measured behavior there. Who is an adult? Someone who refuses to seek stability in the unstable."[37] The subject of the foam world is a deindividuated subject, the collective subject of the working class.

The colonialism of terrestrial globalization entails the deepening of identity roots as they spread throughout and map the world, attempting to produce one united sphere by positioning everything other in relation to the rooted identity. Decolonization fractures this united sphere, as new nations and identities achieve independence, decaying the spread roots. The decolonizing potential of foam rests in its ability to merge independence and interdependence, autonomy, and dependency in shifting ways. In turn, foams help us under-

---

36 Peter Sloterdijk, *Spheres III: Foams: Plural Sphereology*, trans. W. Hoban (Los Angeles: Semiotext(e), 2004/2016), 31.

37 Ibid., 30-31.

stand the contemporaneity of enclosure and openness, showing how grasping and giving-on-and-with can be part of the
same educational praxis. As spatialized self-determinations,
each new bubble is a unique interior in which groups work
on themselves in a protected surround that's both common
and exclusive. The walls of the bubble are shared, and therefore serve to both divide and unite at least two microspheres.
This creates what Sloterdijk refers to as a "paradoxical interi-
or" where "the great majority of surrounding co-bubbles are
simultaneously adjacent and inaccessible, both connected and
removed."[38] Because foam is necessarily acentric, bubble generation reconfigures foam, making new spaces, without appeal
to a central rooted identity.

This kind of generation, to be sure, does not mean that
foams are powerless and ahistorical spheres. Although Sloterdijk's sphereology is not without political deficiencies, he is
certainly aware of and concerned about the historical injustices relative to the distribution of resources in foams, as he
notes that within foam formations today there exist "highly
divergent temperature settings and great inequalities in the
levels of animation, immunization and pampering."[39] And
as Sloterdijk observes at the end of *Globes*, living in thin and
transient walls is not particularly enticing for many people

---

38 Ibid., 54.

39 Ibid., 281. For another example of the progressive potential of
Sloterdijk's sphereology, see Dean Detloff and Matt Bernico, "At-
moterrorism and Atmodesign in the 21st Century: Mediating Flint's
Water Crisis," *Cosmos and History: The Journal of Natural and Social
Philosophy* 13, no. 1 (2017): 156-189.

and groups; in the same way, interdependence might not be as exciting for those without genuine independence. Addressing and alleviating these injustices, however, cannot but take place in the relationships between shared walls of Relation, as "the foam metaphor draws attention to the fact that there are no isolating means which are completely private property—one always shares at least one partition with an adjacent world-cell."[40] The political response must entail the abolition of private property and the redistribution of the resources to comfort those in the colonized world.

It might seem contradictory to discuss walls within Relation. Glissant certainty does not discuss walls, opting instead for vectors and arrows. Yet I maintain that walls are crucial to affirming his historical sensitivity of Relation. This is most apparent in his concern for languages of Relation, which mix and intermingle but are not subsumed into an indeterminate mixture. It is what he calls "the implacable consensus among powers between profits and controls" that moves this subsumption forward. "Not every disappearance, however, is equivalent."[41] In the same way, not all foamed walls are equivalent, and we have to distinguish those that "become foreign, monumental and impervious to empathy," and that "only a privileged few succeed in assigning them to an interior of their own."[42] Walls differ in their history, quality, orientation, aspiration, and duration, and we can posit a relation between

---

40 Sloterdijk, *Spheres III*, 565.

41 Glissant, *Poetics of Relation*, 96.

42 Sloterdijk, *Spheres III*, 214.

these characteristics and the educational processes engaged in foam construction. Foam walls constructed through the grasping of lordly imagining aim for permanence and an exclusive expansion, while the thin walls constructed through errant learning presuppose their ephemerality even as they expand, enlarging only to pop.

Errant learning—as an educational practice that abjures any ultimate and decisive transparency—constructs foams without any solid foundation or final ground. The reason the foam appears white in the open boat's wake is, after all, because this opacity reflects the light of the sun; it's not that the foam is white, but that we cannot see inside the foam, which remains withdrawn and uncoverable. Produced through the contradictory relations of co-division and co-isolation, life in bubbled foams assumes a fundamental opacity:

> Every point in the foam offers glimpses of the bordering ones, but comprehensive views are not available—in the most advanced case, exaggerations are formulated inside one bubble and can be used in many neighboring ones… For theory that accepts being-in-foam as the primary definition of our situation, final super-visions of the One World are not only unattainable, but impossible—and, correctly understood, also undesirable.[43]

Totality is unimaginable and ungraspable. The bubble walls represent a border zone between the known and unknown, the truth and its outside: "truth is neither a secure store of

---

43 Ibid., 58.

facts nor a mere property of statements, but rather a coming and going, a current thematic flashing-up and a sinking into the athematic night."[44] One knows the same wall but not of what lies on the other side. When the wall collapses, something new is known—like, perhaps, who and what lived beyond the wall—but because of the collapse something else is lost, irrecoverable, and forever unknowable. The resulting configuration of foam, accordingly, occasions a fresh Relation to live in and learn.

When bubbles burst, the "air returns home to the general atmosphere while more solid substance disintegrates into drops of dust. What is almost nothing becomes what is almost not."[45] Rather than ground, the air is the element that sustains foam. The heavy gives way to the light. Atlas' sunken shoulders, burdened with the weight of the orb, no longer point to any access to truth. Sloterdijk refers to this process as uplift: "Anti-gravity can now be understood as a 'fundamental' vector, or rather as the tendency that strives against the dimension of a foundation."[46] As bubbles inflate, they move outward and upward in expanse, rather than down through filiation. This is both a reality and a project: "While realistic seriousness has always purported to be and to know what is the case, future realistic thought must start from the realization that anti-gravity is more serious than anything ever formulated about the

---

44 Ibid., 399.

45 Ibid., 29.

46 Ibid., 687.

supposedly 'fundamental' by the consensus."[47] The right to opacity entails a pedagogical struggle against rootedness, an educational project that can move beyond the limits of colonialism by escaping the colonial framework while attending to the historicity of power. The move to the air is not a move away from the claims to land that remain central to struggles against colonialism, settler-colonialism, and imperialism.

The Windbag: An Errant Conclusion

On my reading, lordly imagining is a grasping drive that thickens and fastens ever-expansive walls. Militating against those forces that still possess monospheric intentions requires different forms of imagination and understanding. It is for these purposes that I've offered the pedagogy of errant learning. Errant learning grasps from the impossibility of any final grasping movement in which all is revealed and known, constructing bubbles in foams that move forward only to change. After the circumnavigation of the globe becomes routine, life as foam construction extends horizontally, composing and re-composing Relation. As such, errant learning in foams is not about growing up into adulthood but growing outward into childhood again and again, re-calibrating the fluctuating air conditions of bubbled foam, air that necessarily has to come from the outside and that, after a time, will return to the outside. Learning in and for foams must be errant for this reason: there are no secure trajectories or proper courses to follow.

One figure of the errant learner is the windbag. On a set of bagpipes, the windbag is the skin that fills, holds, and expels the air that channels through the chanter reeds and drones to produce sound. As a pejorative subject, the windbag is someone through whom air passes to vocalize without meaningful content. This is similar to but distinct from the boaster (through whom "hot air" passes as they pump themselves up in front of others) and the actual bagpiper (whose agency determines the flow of air to achieve predetermined tones, pitches, cadences, and so on). The windbag, on the contrary, is a pneumatic envelope with openings that allow it to inflate and deflate. Yet this does not intimate that the windbag is without meaning, intention, or politics: the content that passes through the windbag works to determine—in a non-determining manner—its form and substance. The windbag grasps for air that, although it will pass before any absorption or assimilation takes place, will still give sustaining shape to it for a certain duration. As an errant learner, the windbag follows educational content, creating temporary enclosures in a pneumatic exodus of expanse; temporary presentations waiting for the interruption of inquiry.

3
——————

ERRANT LITERACY IN THE ZONE

In his later works, Jean-François Lyotard identified a new prevailing mode of urbanism that he termed the megalopolis, which has its origins in the city and the town-country relationship and resulted in part from the expansion of the city. This augmentation was not the domination of the city over the rest of the territory such that the outskirts and countryside became the city, but rather the incorporation of the territory into the megalopolis' expansive logic such that the city is no longer a unique coherent region. The megalopolis, then, is not a spatial form but a spatial process, an indeterminate zone that "does not have an exterior and an interior, being both one and the other together."[1] The expansive logic at work here is that of development and efficiency, a logic organized by the

---

1 Jean-François Lyotard, *Postmodern Fables*, trans. G.V.D. Abbeele (Minneapolis: University of Minnesota Press, [1993] 1997), 24.

principle of exchange. This principle, which the megalopolis owes to the economic and political city, is what allows the megalopolis to consume the city, the suburbs, and the country, as all differences between and within each, are rendered fungible. Just as important in this lineage is the zone, which denotes "a belt, neither country nor city, but another site, one not mentioned in the registry of places."[2] The zone, lodged between the city and its outside, was the sphere through which the principle spread until there was only exchange. The megalopolis is the urban *process*, and the zone is the urban *form* and *style* the process generates. While the zone was once an unnamed yet distinct wayward and errant place as opposed to the named and ordered regime of the city, the operations of the megalopolis overcome the distinction through a kind of blurring that mobilizes the wayward and errant properties under the regime of development. If the zone was an indistinct place, it was only because of its relationship to the city and the country.

One paper probes the contours of the megalopolis in relation to what it conquered: the *domus*, a form of domestic community or common, the household, under a monad of "space, time and body under the regime (of) nature."[3] There's a sense of belonging in which exclusions are not necessary. Here, language, life, and association are rhythmical and progressive, meaning they are both developmental and repetitive.

---

2 Ibid., 18.

3 Jean-François Lyotard, *The Inhuman: Reflections on Time*, trans. G. Bennington and R. Bowlby (Stanford: Stanford University Press, [1988] 1991), 191-92.

It's a rhythm of constant and spontaneous work at the service of nature. The child is one such form of rhythm, work, and the natural: "Within the domestic rhythm, it is the moment, the suspension of beginning again, the seed. It is what will have been. It is the surprise, the story starting over again. Speechless, *infans*, it will babble, speak, tell stories, will have told stories, will have stories told about it, will have had stories told about it."[4] Under the domus, the child is a fresh beginning that ensures continuity and repetition, that which maintains coherence through the possibility of beginning again. At the same time, and because of this, the child enacts the interruptions and excesses of the domus. There can be no domestic community without something to domesticate. The domestic rhythm does not suture or heal interruptions, but '*scars* over' them.[5] Neither suppressed nor absorbed, unpredictable and unintelligible disruptions are simply a structural part of the natural realm under—and for—which humans produce their domiciles. Nature, impossible to subject to cognition, is fate.

Lyotard tells us that he can only write about the *domus* from within the megalopolis, an urban form of community that's not based on a relation to nature but to exchange. There's no more memory, narrative, or rhythm, just databanks and algorithms. The megalopolis is the geographic manifestation of what he terms 'the system,' which operates according to the logic of performativity where, driven by the demand to maximize the efficiency of inputs and outputs, "everyone seeks and will find as best s/he can the information needed to

---

4 Ibid., 193.

5 Ibid., 192.

make a living, which makes no sense."[6] The megalopolis has replaced the order of the *domus*, broken apart its rhythmic and spatial belonging to introduce a process of communication and commerce between individuals. In the place of an order dictated by the mystery of nature, it installs a democratic and capitalist system based on reason, rationality, and exchange. The system prohibits mystery and interruption not through repression or exclusion, but incorporation and development. Everything can and must be brought within its structure.

The spokespeople of the megalopolis tell us that this is progress and justice. By making everything transparent and communicable, by bringing the *domus* inside, we can resolve all problems, address all wrongs, repair all divisions. Such inclusion, however, ultimately works to transform the untamable interruptions that pervaded the *domus*: "What domesticity regulated—savagery—it demanded. It had to have its off-stage within itself."[7] Whereas the *domus*, haunted by interruptions, accepts opacity *qua* opacity, the megalopolis consumes interruptions, rendering opacity as nothing more than unrealized transparency. This consumption is fundamental to its development: "Secrets must be put into circuits, writings programmed, tragedies transcribed into bits of information… The secret is capitalized swiftly and efficiently."[8] There is no service to mystery, no submission to interruptions that would compel us to construct a domicile. There is no need for

---

6 Ibid., 194.

7 Ibid., 201.

8 Ibid.

shelter without the threat of the untamable, and the zone's internal spatial divisions are inessential, being merely rooms in a massive museum that can shift, collapse, or emerge as more objects accumulate. What is essential is "the multiplicity of competing figures," which provides the megalopolis with 'an air of critique thanks to the comparison possible between 'good objects.'"[9]

Here we can approach the pedagogical apparatus that accompanies and facilitates the spread of the megalopolis. To compare is to subject different objects to a common measure and is predicated upon according or giving a form to something. In according a form, something is placed under an existing category or concept, while in giving a form, a new category or concept is created. Both "forms and concepts are constitutive of objects, they pro-duce data that can be grasped by sensibility and that are intelligible to the understanding."[10] This pedagogy of *grasping* is the motor of the megalopolis, which positions everything as a potential object to be known and exchanged. Under the *domus*, the child is both a child and a future adult, a something and a someone. Simultaneously an interruption into and a legitimation of continuity, the *domus* serves the child. In the megalopolis, the child is merely a deficient adult, one that does not need to be tamed but needs to be developed by grasping, through which the child learns how to grasp as it is grasped. The child or the student is not some*thing* that *will* speak (as in the *domus*), but some*one* that *can* and *must* speak.

---

9 Lyotard, *Postmodern Fables*, 27.

10 Lyotard, *The Inhuman*, 140.

The methods and contents—the information, knowledge, politics, habits, or beliefs they represent—are (largely) irrelevant. While specific instances of grasping are guided by specific ends, grasping itself is a never-ending process, a constant development that never stops for the individuals of the megalopolis as we expand the museum. In the university of the megalopolis, it is less significant *what* one grasps and more important that one learns *how* to grasp. This accounts for the refrain of administrators, admissions counselors, and public relations officers: we are preparing students not just for jobs that do not yet exist, but for an entire world that does not yet exist. By "world," they mean the specific internal configuration of the museum, which does not yet exist because it is the object of endless development, an end in itself, an end without any end.

The flexibility and openness of the megalopolis correspond with that of its pedagogy. Anything and everything is only a new possibility to be realized, a new unknown to be grasped. How exciting! Even the worst of problems can be accommodated, for each new dispute or tragedy "requires new regulations, other forms of community that must be invented."[11] Every x is exchangeable and capable of entering into the circuits of the megalopolis, and if an x is not so at the present moment, then through grasping it will be so in the future, at which point it will be placed, compared, and evaluated alongside the other objects in the museum. This will happen efficiently through the individualization and diversification of learning styles, objectives, outcomes, assessments,

---

11 Lyotard, *Postmodern Fables*, 31.

and evaluations. Any gap between possibility and actuality must be bridged by the imaginary as quickly as possible. Nothing is outside the power of imagination or the mind's ability to grasp. Everything is directed toward the individual of the megalopolis, in need of decipherment and comparison.

If Lyotard can only write what he does about the *domus* from within the megalopolis, it's not because it was a previous, empirically definable stage of history that demands a distance for comprehension. He doubts it ever really existed as a form of community. Instead, it has to do with the very struggle over pedagogical relations, and the resistance to grasping in and for the zone. There is always something that resists development: the *domus*, which exists within the megalopolis as the force of impossibility, which "is not only the opposite of *possible*, it is a case of it, the *zero* case of possibility."[12] The way to inhabit the megalopolis is "by citing the lost *domus*,"[13] by inhabiting the zero case of childhood's possibility. The *domus* exists as "the child whose awakening displaces it to the future horizon of his thoughts and writing, to a coming which will always have to be deferred."[14] Childhood—which is linked with thought and writing—includes but is more than a beginning and passing stage of life, and also refers to a recurrent state that runs counter to and interrupts development. Biological childhood is when the human is in-human, when we're radically dependent on others yet without the capacity or means to recog-

---

12 Lyotard, *The Inhuman*, 197.

13 Ibid., 200.

14 Ibid., 201.

nize, account for, or respond to this dependency. The child is not a human yet because there is no "I" that can speak. As a recurrent state, childhood or infancy is an interruption in the subject's humanity, in which we cannot participate in the debate, dialogue, reason, or exchange that is so essential to the megalopolis. The child is, in short, stupid, and the stupidity of the child is the pedagogical stake of marxist education in the zone.[15]

Illiteracy in the Zone

The trajectory of development in grasping proceeds from ignorance to knowledge. Ignorance is the possibility of communicable and exchangeable knowledge. Through grasping, ignorance develops into competent and articulate knowledge. Ignorance, like grasping, is always active, constantly on the move toward mastery, destined for its proper place amongst "the billions of padded messages" in "the immense zone."[16] Stupidity, which can never be developed, threatens this trajectory. As Lyotard defines it at one point, it is "a no-saying amid the always already said."[17] Such a no-saying is not the refusal to speak—which would necessitate the *ability* to speak—but the very impotence and failure of speech, its permanent opacity. It is only, Lyotard writes, in a state of stupor that we can access this impotent energy, "because it consists only in the

---

15 For a marxist take on stupidity and revolution, see Derek R. Ford, *Marxism, Pedagogy, and the General Intellect: Beyond the Knowledge Economy* (New York: Palgrave Macmillan, 2021), 75-89.

16 Lyotard, *Postmodern Fables*, 31.

17 Lyotard, *The Inhuman*, 202.

timbre of a sensitive, sentimental matter."[18]

Organized around the pedagogy of grasping, the zone's museum has "no need for writing, childhood, pain" because it is "an economy in which everything is taken, nothing received. And so necessarily, an illiteracy."[19] There is no service or surrender to the untamable, no obligation to live with interruptions. Childhood as recurrent inhumanity and writing are inessential to the megalopolis because they cannot factor into an exchange. They are relegated to the zone's ghettos, which are not planned by the metropolis as spatially distinct areas, but instead are the result of "prodigal thought" that "*secretes* the wall of its ghetto."[20] The ghetto walls are the discharge of the secret, marks of stupor that cannot be grasped. Illiteracy, on this reading, is not the negation or suppression of literacy, but instead a development of literacy as grasping, through which forms and concepts constitute objects under the mind's direction and the subject's will. These traces are what the megalopolis could do without and are the reason it tries to develop the child as quickly as possible. They are also what can open an alternative pedagogy to grasping, which I want to sketch by turning to some of Lyotard's writing on writing and sound, to gesture toward an errant literacy.

In his letter ostensibly addressed to David Rogozinski, Lyotard comments on Claude Lefort's analysis of George Orwell's *1984*. What Lyotard finds significant is, first, that

---

18 Ibid., 201.

19 Ibid., 199.

20 Ibid., 200.

Orwell's book is not a work of criticism but literature. Criticism, as we have seen, is perfectly acceptable to, and even desirable for, the megalopolis. The kind of writing Lyotard is after is one that "demands privation" and thus "cannot cooperate with a project of domination or total transparency, even involuntarily."[21] Orwell's hero, Winston, writes the novel not as a manifesto or theoretical excursus, but as a private diary, an act that begins as a resistance through which Winston encounters his "secret universe."[22] Yet as he writes his innermost thoughts—driven by an attempt to escape the system—he *articulates the secret*, obliterating it and facilitating its swift and efficient capture in the megalopolis. The capture and defense of the secret hinges on the relation between language and writing, which are both allied and opposed to each other. "One writes against language, but necessarily with it. To say what it already knows how to say is not writing. One wants to say what it does not know how to say, but what one imagines it should be able to say."[23] We can only write *with* language, but we *present with* language to move beyond or outside of it into the secret life of *inquiry*.[24]

21 Jean-François Lyotard, *The Postmodern Explained: Correspondence 1982-1985*, trans. D. Barry, B. Maher, J. Pefanis, V. Spate, and M. Thomas (Minneapolis: University of Minnesota Press, [1988] 1993), 88.

22 Ibid.

23 Ibid., 89.

24 For more on Lyotard and the communist project, see Ford, *Communist Study*, 67-90.

When the secret is absorbed into the megalopolis through articulation, writing is subsumed by language. But this domination is never really total as long as writing takes place because writing is "one region where restlessness, lack, and 'idiocy' come out into the open."[25] This is the childish stupidity that emerges through writing, which always indicates there is something that language cannot capture, that cannot be reduced to information. There seems to be a kind of writing that's most open to stupidity, which he finds in Walter Benjamin's writings on childhood, which do not *describe* childhood but indicate "the childhood of the event and inscribe what is uncapturable about it."[26] In describing childhood, I might seek to articulate something new about childhood, to show how it's unique. But this would remain tied to the megalopolis' logic of development, in which an event is transformed into an innovation, something new that can be sold or circulated throughout the infinite exchange routes of the megalopolis. Each innovation is a child that has grown up. Instead, childish reading-writing is about an *initiation* into childhood; an unknown that remains unknown and only appears through traces. Instead of the diary, the more appropriate act of resistance in the novel is the production of idiom, singular words that cannot be translated or transferred that articulate that which cannot be captured and, in so doing, never quite succeeds at signaling what it names. Because the idiom always fails, it's the experience of initiation without development. The idiom is singular but also shared, a common point of

---

25 Lyotard, *The Postmodern Explained*, 90.

26 Ibid.

contact in which we share in the secret. In love, there is "the never-ending search for a different idiom of sensibility, this vertigo where my idiom and yours falter, where they look for exchange, where they resist and discover each other."[27] The idiom is never complete, can never capture what it wants, and hence cannot grow up into an innovation, destined always and only to the experience of initiation.

The megalopolis is not reducible to the totalitarian system in *1984*, but what the two share in common is the reduction of writing to language. The megalopolis does not seek to eliminate writing, but to translate its singularity as an initiation that *must* grow up into an innovation. Lyotard will later affirm this after the triumph of the liberal-capitalist-imperialist system, which did so precisely because it was *open* to writing, it *needed* writing and the secret, without which there would be nothing new to inscribe in its circuits. But it needs a particular kind of writing: innovative writing, adult writing, transparent writing.

Writing and Listening to the Silent Teaching of Words

In several texts, particularly after he began writing about sound and music, Lyotard introduces a sonic dimension to literacy. In "Address on the Subject of the Course of Philosophy," for example, he linked philosophical literacy to listening. Because philosophy is not an object or a corpus of knowledge, but rather the activity of thinking and questioning, philosophical literacy is "an exercise in discomposure in relation to the text, an exercise in patience," the patience of never being done reading, discovering "that you have not read what you have

---

27 Ibid., 92.

read," such that "reading is an exercise in listening." [28] In a short foreword to a collection of his works, which later appeared in *Postmodern Fables*, Lyotard introduces three aesthetic dynamics of literacy, which each correspond to a particular kind of writing.

First, there is *hearing* writing. When you hear yourself write "you hear only something that has to be written," are confident in the writing, "ahead" of it. [29] Hearing writing is a transparent communication between sound and text, the words in the head and the words on the page, where language and writing are allies. You're confident that you're writing what you're hearing. Second, there is *listening* writing, which is uncertain writing, when you hesitate to write because of the suspension or gap between what you hear and what you write. This hesitation can lead in two directions. On one hand, you might "strap it down, make it severe, classical, academic," arguing your points against another; on the other hand, it can also lead to a neglect of the writing. [30] If you're uncertain, that is, you might disrespect the adherence of writing to language insofar as the links between the two are lost. This ambiguity ensures that you'll have to continue to listen to the writing, continue to write again. Third, there is *not listening* writing. You're not listening to the writing, but *for* something else entirely, beyond reading and thinking through words and language: "You lend

---

28 Ibid., 101.

29 Lyotard, *Postmodern Fables*, 149.

30 Ibid., 150

an ear only to what comes along."[31]

We can take these distinctions as different relations to thought with different temporalities. Hearing writing is a correspondence to formulations, or an immediate harmonization between language and writing. Listening writing is an interruption in the harmony, one that desynchronizes language and writing, thought and articulation. The relationship between thought and articulation is suspended, ambiguous, and unsettled, but still present nonetheless Not listening writing is a sonic openness to the present or an obedience to noise. Meaning is absent and without any relation to the writing. The reason why Lyotard ascribes illiteracy to the megalopolis is that it is organized solely around hearing and listening. There is only information to be exchanged and knowledge to be produced. You can hesitate, yes, as long as you produce something intelligible. There is not a hierarchy of values within the three modes of sonic writing, however; it is not as if hearing and listening must be resisted. In fact, the three modes might be either heterogeneously blocked together or viewed along a continuum. Like childhood, thought is recurrent, is within and beyond formulation, an encounter with inquiry. But it is through not listening that the inquiring child is birthed. The child does not hear words, but noise. The words are still there of course, but they are unrecognizable, indeterminable, without any links or chains between them. They are words as not-words, words as charges, affects, or mute matter.

Because the mute word cannot be developed, one cannot learn to listen or not listen to writing. We can only learn hear-

---

31 Ibid.

ing writing. This is, in part, because we can *know* what hearing writing is: there are words, they mean things, and these meanings can be ordered, interpreted, and deciphered. This is the writing of the megalopolis, in which all differences and initiations are only new variables to be named, rendered transparent, and circulated. What is an appropriate pedagogical mode for the other sonic forms of literacy? If they're not learned, then how can they be taught?

A marxist teaching of errant literacy is a paradoxical pursuit in which teachers and students "suspend the activity of comparing and grasping" in order "to become open to the invasion of nuances, passible to timbre."[32] This requires "a mindless state of mind, which is required of mind not for matter to be perceived or conceived, given or grasped, but *so that there be* some something."[33] Literacy here entails an inversion of the current relationship between the subject and words. In the zone, the subject is the one who grasps words and, through composition, appropriates and exploits words. In errant literacy, we are the subjects of words. But words are not there *for* us to use, to inspire us, or allow us to accord or give form. After all, "words want nothing. They are the 'un-will', the 'non-sense' of thought, its mass."[34] The excess of the word relative to meaning and signification is not a challenge that should or can be overcome. The lesson their disobedience teaches us is our obedience to the process of

---

32 Lyotard, *The Inhuman*, 139.

33 Ibid., 140.

34 Ibid., 142.

inquiry. Hearing writing casts the excess aside as it must *present* the argument while listening writing flirts with excess, and not listening writing allows the secrets of the words to do their work, to subject us to the recessive sway of inquiry. To be passible to the matter of words, however, is not to be passive. It is not a matter of teachers and students throwing up their hands and surrendering the university to words. The writer still picks up the pen or places their hands on the keyboard. Presentation, ultimately, takes place—although it is pricked by silent and inaudible inquiry.

Rather than *present* what this kind of marxist literacy is, I'll instead offer two examples. The first is from Lyotard's second book on André Malraux. Lyotard writes that Malraux's writing is "a writing at the limit of writing."[35] Limit writing, which he also terms *absolute* writing, is done under the sovereignty of the word, is an act that "is authorized by no voice, aims at no end."[36] Writing, in other words, is done to write, to express the *fact* of writing, and to change this *fact* into an *artifact*. The fact is an action, a charge of matter that guides writing, which seizes on and disarticulates the written words to produce the artifact, its objectification that still contains a signal or energy within it. Malraux teaches us this through his conception and deployment of ellipses, on which, Malraux says, "all art

---

35 Jean-François Lyotard, *Soundproof Room: Malraux's Anti-Aesthetics*, trans. R. Harvey (Stanford: Stanford University Press, [1993] 2001), 10.

36 Ibid., 32.

is grounded."[37] The ellipses are an anacoluthon that enacts or signals the incompletion and failure of a sentence. In doing so, it "imposes silence on the verbiage of intrigues and allows to murmur the mutism that it covers."[38] We might think, first of all, of the ellipses as an "etcetera," or that which indicates an addition of words to a phrase, which are thereby included through their exclusion. While we might assume their exclusion stems from our reasonable assumption of what comes next, there is no way of confirming even the most standard and routine linkages. The etcetera not only signals an indeterminate and infinite number of words, but also remains mute as to their linkages. It follows that the meaning of the articulated presentation is likewise suspended or rendered ungraspable through errantry.

The second example comes from Lewis' reading of Althusser's writing, and in particular "his distinctive use of italicization." Althusser's constant use of italics, Lewis suggests, is the literary "equivalent of the swerve, shifting a word ever so slightly so as to highlight it, bring out its meaning, curve the reader's eye toward a nuanced inflection. Such a gesture is both formal and philosophical but also *pedagogical* (notice my italicized swerve here). It is about attentiveness to this word and not that word."[39] As a marxist teacher, Althusser is as-

37 André Malraux, cited in Jean-François Lyotard, *Signed, Malraux*, trans. R. Harvey (Minneapolis: University of Minnesota Press, [1996] 1999), 87.

38 Ibid., 62.

39 Tyson E. Lewis, "Afterword: Studying the Dross," in D. Backer, *The Gold and the Dross*, 78-79.

sembling an encounter with *this* element to see what might take hold if we study it for the inaudible matter of the word. I'd add that the italics represent an *errant* opening to disinterpellation in which we're subject to the passing charge of the openness of inquiry in the same way that Althusser's "scare quotes" create a margin around the words and prevent any firm links between the words inside and outside to be drawn. While we can produce uncertain connections ("what is it about *'this'* word?"), these always slip out of our grasp. Set within and apart by the scare quotes, the words "attack" the text and the reader, as we're rendered passible to the nuance and timbre of the word that "*differ* and *defer*," preventing our identification of a word with a meaning.[40]

Scare quotes "interrupt" the text, the reader, and the writer, disindividuating our subjectivity. Within, against, and beyond the chatter of the megalopolis where, through exchange, errant literacy establishes a zone between words that is neither inside nor outside of the word. As readers and writers subjected to the limit, we're stupefied and interrupted, drawn to the timbre and nuance of the word, which we can only try to think. The errant matter of words comes from that according to which I do not matter, and passes through me, leading me elsewhere but not developing me. A secret pedagogy secreted onto foam walls.

---

40 Lyotard, *The Inhuman*, 140.

4

POSTDIGITAL MARXIST ENCOUNTERS

The zone is a postdigital space, in which the opposition between the analog and digital—like that between the megalopolis and the *domus*—is not so much overcome as it is errantly suspended and moved to a different political and pedagogical terrain. As Curry Malott shows, the postdigital is, as so many definitions put it, difficult to pin down. The reason is that the postdigital is a *dialectical* process; it is "something *real*, something in perpetual motion, something in the process of development, and something sublated."[1] The postdigital is the sublation of the analog under the digital, as the former continues to exist but in a reconfigured form or, more precisely, in a constantly *reshaping* form. The struggle, as Malott formulates it, is over *what form the postdigital will take*, which will be determined by *what mode of production prevails*. This struggle is what this chapter builds on by returning to analog marxists

---

1 Curry Malott, "Capitalism, Crisis, and Educational Struggle in the Postdigital," *Postdigital Science and Education* 1, no. 2 (2019): 372.

to discuss the technological foundations on which the communist mode of production will arise and their relationships to production, knowledge, research, and subjectivity; in short, the "general intellect."

As we saw in the introduction, proletarians produce the knowledge and innovations that make technological changes possible. Yet we do not recognize them as doing such. As Marx formulated it, "in machinery, objectified labour confronts living labour within the labour process itself as the power which rules it; a power which, as the appropriation of living labour, is the form of capital."[2] The general intellect is, for Marx, precisely such a process of real subjection through the objectification of knowledge in technology. The general intellect—which Marx introduces in the *Grundrisse* notebooks—is "the accumulation of knowledge and of skill, of the general productive forces of the social brain" which are "absorbed into capital, as opposed to labour, and hence appears as an attribute of capital."[3] This is from a section of the *Grundrisse* labeled—in the 1960s—the "Fragment on Machines."

In the Fragment, Marx concentrates on some of the contradictory aspects of the ongoing development and dispersion of machinery, especially as they relate to what he called the organic composition of capital. Capital, for Marx, is not just an economic system but a dynamic social and political one as well. This meant he had different ways of looking at how capital was composed, like those introduced at the beginning of chapter 25 of volume 1. One is the technical composition

---

2 Marx, *Grundrisse*, 693.

3 Ibid., 694.

of capital, which is the ratio between the number of workers employed and the number of means of production (machines, raw materials, etc.) they work on. Another is the value
composition of capital, which is the ratio of the *value* of labor
power and the *value* of the means of production. The first is
quantitative and the second is qualitative. There's a relationship between the two, and the organic composition of capital
names this relationship as changes in the second are brought
about by changes in the former. That is to say, if the number
of machines increases while the number of workers decreases
because the machinery is more productive, this will cause the
value composition of capital to change, as there will be less
labor power employed and more means of production used.

As capital develops, "the creation of real wealth comes
to depend less on labour time… but depends rather on the
general state of science and the progress of technology, or
the application of this science to production."[4] Technological
transformations tell us "to what degree general social knowledge has become a *direct force of production*, and to what degree, hence, the conditions of the process of social life itself
have come under the control of the general intellect and been
transformed in accordance with it."[5] This presents or intensifies two contradictory tendencies inherent in capitalism. The
first is the "falling rate of profit." As profit is the ratio of
surplus-value divided by variable capital (wages) and constant
capital (including machinery), as investments in machinery (as
the congealed general intellect) grows, the rate of profit falls

4 Ibid., 704-705.

5 Ibid., 706.

(because machines do not produce value but merely transfer their existing value). Marx takes this up later in the third volume of *Capital*. The second contradiction, which is related to the first, has to do with the source and measurement of value. Rather than surplus labor power driving production, it is the appropriation of the general intellect, "the development of the social individual which appears as the great foundation-stone of production and of wealth."[6] Thus, the general intellect—congealed in machinery—he writes (again, in notebooks not intended for publication) provides "the material conditions to blow this foundation sky-high."[7] Of course, material *conditions* are not *guarantees*, and capitalism for Marx cannot abolish itself through its contradictions; only the class struggle can do that—partially by analyzing and using these contradictions for its purposes.

At this point, it's necessary to define what exactly machinery is in the world of capital because we can then see why this debate about the general intellect and its location and relations is so important. In the second volume of *Capital* Marx categorizes machinery as *fixed capital*, which is distinct from *circulating* capital. Both are *forms* of capital in the production process. Circulating capital physically circulates along with the commodity. For example, the cotton used to produce a t-shirt enters the t-shirt and circulates with it. At the same time, however, "another part remains fixed in the means of labour and hence in the production process. The value fixed in this way steadily declines, until the means of labour is worn out and

---

6 Ibid., 705.

7 Ibid., 706.

has therefore distributed its value, in a longer or shorter period, over the volume of products that has emerged from a series of continually repeated labour processes."[8] While much fuss is made today about the *mobility* of capital–which can certainly move about the globe like never before—this tendency toward mobility exists alongside a contradictory tendency toward immobility. Take, for example, the revolutions in transportation and communication, which arise to overcome the barriers capital encounters as it expands throughout space and time. Capitalism constantly works to produce a set of spatial relations that enable production and circulation to happen as quickly as possible. Selling time is particularly important in this regard. This is why Malott proposes that capitalist crises in the postdigital era tend to manifest as crises of *realization*.

A permanently effective cause "in differentiating the times of selling, and thus the periods of turnover in general, is the distance of the market in which a commodity is sold from its place of production."[9] This is another motivating force behind capital's drive to annihilate space by time, and developments in transportation are fundamental to this. "The improvement of the means of communication and transportation cuts down absolutely the wandering period of the commodities but does not eliminate the relative difference in the time of circulation of different commodity-capitals aris-

---

8 Karl Marx, *Capital: A Critique of Political Economy (Vol. 2): The Process of Circulation of Capital* (New York: International Publishers, 1885/1967), 158.

9 Ibid., 249.

ing from their peregrinations."[10] As a result, "the velocity of movement in space accelerated and thereby the geographic distance shortened in time."[11] Developments in communication help coordinate advances in transportation.

Two contradictory implications arise from these concurrent developments. The first implication is that the overall mass of commodities circulating through space and time increases and, as a result, there is a greater outlay of capital that is locked in commodity form. The second implication is that there is a greater outlay of capital invested in transportation and communication. These are contradictory developments because, while advances in transportation and communication are intended to—and, in many ways, do—help facilitate the realization of value, by increasing the outlay of capital the risk of crisis is heightened and intensified (the risk of crisis by devaluation, for example).

Fixed capital is not an accidental but a necessary form of capital; it comes about as a direct consequence of capital's logic. Like all elements of capitalism, fixed capital is quite a contradiction in that it is, well, fixed, while capital is all about motion and fluidity—the *expansion* and movement of value. Fixed capital is resolutely necessary for capital, however: "Fixed capital is as much a presupposition for the production of circulating capital as circulating capital is for the production of fixed capital."[12] Don Mitchell makes the significance

---

10 Ibid.

11 Ibid., 249-250.

12 Marx, *Grundrisse*, 734.

of this antagonism explicit: "For capital to be free," he writes, "it must also be fixed in place" and this represents "the central geographic contradiction of capitalism."[13] One way that capital attempts to deal with this contradiction is, not surprisingly, through ideology. By touting itself as infinitely mobile and able to leap across the globe at the drop of a dime, capital can dictate a range of local policies and practices.

Postdigital Communism and Pedagogy:
Beyond Measure?

The extent to which the general intellect is the driving motor of production and knowledge is central to economics, politics, and the world generally, poses several problems for capital. At the same time, then, it poses numerous possibilities for resistance; namely that knowledge is non-rivalrous, non-exclusive, and does not operate according to the logic of scarcity. For one, knowledge does not always or readily take the form of a commodity over which one can claim private ownership. It's easier to claim a plot of land, a building, a set of machines, or a batch of raw materials than it is to claim knowledge. As a result, the status of knowledge as a public or private good is hard to ascribe. Knowledge does not obey the same laws of scarcity or rivalry as physical commodities. One person's knowledge does not eliminate the possibility of another person's knowledge except through capitalist enclosure and expropriation. When one person utilizes knowledge, it's not as if the knowledge is diminished for or inaccessible

---

13 Don Mitchell, *The Right to the City: Social Justice and the Fight for Public Space* (New York: The Guilford Press, 2003), 165.

to another. Moreover, the more people access knowledge the more knowledge can be created. Finally, because it's hard to draw boundaries around knowledge and designate it as a commodity, it's also difficult to prevent people from accessing knowledge. Everyone on the political spectrum, from the neoliberals to the marxists, acknowledges this.

Some contemporary marxist theorists believe that the predominance of the general intellect undercuts Marx's theory of value, precisely because you cannot measure the labor time for the production of communication, affects, language, knowledge, and so on. Yet Marx's law of value is precisely *immeasurable*. For Marx, value is socially-necessary labor time, which he called so because 1) it is the overall average time it takes to produce a commodity (e.g., if it takes me two days to produce the same commodity that you produce in one day, my commodity is not twice as valuable and instead, if we are the only producers, the socially-necessary labor time for our commodity would be exactly in the middle at 1.5 days); and 2) it fulfills a need or desire of society at the time (if I produce a commodity that no one wants, the labor embodied in it has no value because there is no use value; it's literally a non-value). Both aspects of value are dynamic; they change over time and in ways that are often unpredictable and hard to pinpoint at the moment. The utility of anything is qualitative and singular, so it escapes not only measure but even the consciousness of the consumer (don't we all wonder why we get enjoyment out of certain things—television shows, singers, etc.?).

The real question is not about measure. Instead, as Malott formulates it properly, it is "how to sublate ourselves, and the world in the process, into a world of non-alienated cyborgs, free of exploitation, building a still opaque communist future."[14] Hardt and Negri helpfully remind us that there is a "mistake in posing an *ontological* division and even opposition between human life and machines. Human thought and action have always been interwoven with techniques and technologies."[15] The division between fixed capital and living labor is a *class* division, not an ontological one, and should be treated as a political struggle as Malott asserts. The division between the digital and the analog is historical and political. The immeasurable is a weapon in the class struggle, one that is up for grabs by the two classes engaged in struggle.

Postdigital Capitalism *or* Postdigital Communism

Interestingly, neither Marx nor Lenin ever write about a *socialist* mode of production. Instead, Lenin defines socialism "as the transition between the capitalist mode of production and the communist mode of production."[16] Social formations take various forms and are composed of different modes of production, some or one of which is ascendant or dominant. As a social formation, socialism is the heterogeneity of elements of both modes of production in which communist relations and means of production are ascending through the class struggle. Marx identifies several elements of the communist mode of production in capitalism, from joint-stock companies to the

14 Malott, "Capitalism, Crisis, and Educational Struggle in the Postdigital," 372.

15 Michael Hardt and Antonio Negri, *Assembly* (New York: Oxford University Press, 2017), 109.

16 Althusser, *History and Imperialism*, 63.

general intellect. "They are," Althusser insists, "not all communist elements. They are elements for communism."[17] In the same way, peer collaboration, the general intellect, collective projects, and so on, are also elements for communism. Right now, however, they're captured by capitalism which functions precisely by valorizing the immeasurability that some on the left celebrate.

Marx in the postdigital era does not pose a technical or juridical challenge, but a class challenge: how to collectivize the proletarian class—in practice and theory—to advance the class struggle. As capital produced the collective worker it continually had—and has—to divide us. In the U.S., the primary mode has been division through individuation. This theme runs throughout *A history of education for the many: From colonization and slavery to the decline of US imperialism*, where Malott demonstrates that the common school movement's leaders like Horace Mann argued that common schools would "reorient how workers understand how to improve their conditions. The objective was to replace the view that better working conditions and a better life are achieved through unions and collective struggle with an individualist orientation."[18] Most interestingly, Malott shows how this orientation informed critical pedagogy, a term Henry Giroux coined in the early 1980s that foregrounds "agency in the classroom" and works "at the individual level of micro-politics. Critical

---

17 Ibid., 65.

18 Curry S. Malott, *A History of Education for the Many: From Colonization and Slavery to the Decline of US Imperialism* (London: Bloomsbury, 2021), 90.

pedagogy's most common active subject of change is the individual critically conscious teacher acting for the many rather than with the many."[19]

To move to the many, we have to move beyond the individual subject. Marx dedicates the 1857 Introduction to showing that the *production* of the subject as an individual was a historical product, one that emerged in the 18th century and one that, as such, was far from natural or transcendental. This was his critique of so many bourgeois political economists of his day (as well as Proudhon). For them, the eighteenth-century individual, he writes, "appears as an ideal, whose existence they project into the past. Not as a historical result but as history's point of departure."[20] That the *individual* is the subject of production is "as much of an absurdity as is the development of language without individuals living *together* and talking to each other."[21] This, in addition to the withdrawal of state support and financial precarity, and so on, could provide another reason for why Jodi Dean claims the individual subject-form is failing today. Interestingly, she argues that "the technologies that further individuation … provide at the same time an escape from and an alternative to individuation: connection to others, collectivity."[22] As we take to social media to post our different "takes" on events and articles, we at the same time *repost* those of others. And the singular post is not

---

19   Ibid., 188.

20   Marx, *Grundrisse*, 83.

21   Ibid., 84.

22   Jodi Dean, *Crowds and Party* (New York: Verso, 2016), 64.

what we desire: we're interested in retweets and reposts. She gives an interesting example in an essay on selfies. "In communicative capitalism," Dean writes:

> images of others are images of me. Each day, millions of tweets include text saying "this is me" or "then, I'm like" with an accompanying GIF of someone who is not actually them. I convey who I am by sharing a photo of someone else. My identity or sense of self is not so singular or unique that it can only stand for itself, only represent itself. It's interchangeable with others. Their faces and expressions convey my own. Not only do I see myself in others, I present others as myself. The face that once suggested the identity of a singular person now flows in collective expression of common feelings.[23]

We feel joy as we immerse ourselves in the networks and take part in collective activity. This is a postdigital experience in which the boundaries between our analog and digital embodiments are blurred and ultimately indecipherable. My—our—subjectivity is sensed *materially* and *virtually* at once. Networked technologies are communist elements in our capitalist social formation, the question is how to pedagogically seize such elements so they can take hold.

Yet just as the postdigital blurs the lines between the digital and analog, so too might it blur the lines between the in-

---

23 Jodi Dean, "Faces as Commons: The Secondary Visuality of Communicative Capitalism," *Open!* 31 December 2016. Available at: https://onlineopen.org/faces-as-commons.

dividual and collective, thereby rendering the choice between the two alternatives false. This is the line pursued by Virno and others who, following Marx, insist that "the individual is a *result*, not a presupposition."[24] One cannot understand subjectivity and its relationship to capitalist pedagogy by taking the individual as it is already conceptualized. The individual is the result of a process of *individuation*, which means, in turn, that there's a *pre-individual* stratum of reality, a common and public space from which individuations result.

For Virno, this only "becomes a real possibility… in the age of the technological reproducibility of experience and the absolute centrality of technological-scientific intelligentsia within material production."[25] Under Taylorist production, machinery determines the labor process. "Labor adjusts itself, in a memetic way, to the system of efficient causes: not only does it comply with it but it also interiorizes it in its procedures and lets itself be defined by it."[26] The separation of planning and execution, embedded in machinery at this age, however, is broken under post-Fordism thanks to new digital technologies. Unlike machinery, information technologies "do not produce possible states of affairs, but the formal possibility of as yet undetermined states of affairs," so that they— unlike industrial machines—"do not in any way indicate *what*

---

24 Paolo Virno, *Convention and Materialism*, trans. L. Chiesa (Cambridge: The MIT Press, 1986/2020), 80.

25 Ibid., 81.

26 Ibid., 102.

eventuality will be realized."[27] "The identity between rules for planning and rules for performing," Virno continues, "diminishes the validity of a distinction between the two moments and implies a significant overlapping between intention and realization."[28] The forces of production under contemporary capitalism are a pre-individual, common terrain of individuation.

The classic example of pre-individual commonality "is the way in which crystals are the crystallization of a solution, which is to say the individuation of conditions, compounds, and elements that exist initially in flux," as Jason Read writes in his book on transindividuality.[29] "What is called pre-individual exists," he continues, "primarily as a metastable state, as a set of possibilities and relations" and "individuation is in part the reconciliation of the tensions and potentials of this metastable state."[30] The pre-individual common is not "pre" as in *before* the individuated individual because individuation is never final or complete. Thus, the digital technologies of postdigital capitalist pedagogies provide a pre-individual common syntax from which infinite potential individuations can emerge.

The problem with capitalist postdigital pedagogy is that it limits individuation to the capitalist form of individuality

---

27 Ibid., 68.

28 Ibid., 109.

29 Jason Read, *The Politics of Transindividuality* (Chicago: Haymarket Books, 2015), 109.

30 Ibid.

and reinforces our conception and experience of individuality as a finalized starting point rather than an endpoint. The tracking devices worn by workers and utilized by corporations and schools, for example, limit the process of individuation to a quantifiable and transparent form of subjectivity. The pre-individual resources from which we can draw are owned and controlled by capital rather than people. The political task is thus to wrest such technologies from capital and the pedagogical task is to demonstrate—through practice—the infinite possibilities of individuation. If the human subject does not leave behind its origins as an individual but is continually haunted by them, then postdigital pedagogies against capital find their educational potentiality within such a haunting that permeates every moment.

Such a pedagogy does not reject transparent knowledge—or *presentation*—but augments it with the opacity of *thought*—or with *inquiry*—thereby affirming Han's assertion that "in contrast to calculation, thinking is not transparent."[31] Calculation requires surveillance, data collection, postdigital personalized and customizable devices. It reduces students and teachers and all of us to *individuals* via numerical inputs and outputs. Organized around the demand for actualization, calculation produces transparent *knowledge*. Capitalist pedagogy is structured around visibility and transparent knowledge, which reinforces the capitalist requirement to eliminate all *distance*, the demand that guides postdigital educational technologies and pedagogies. "Illumination is exploitation. Overexposing

31 Byung-Chul Han, *The Transparency Society* (Stanford: Stanford University Press, 2015), 30.

individual subjects maximizes economic efficiency," as Han writes.[32] Instead of differentiating calculation from thinking, the pedagogical demand is to differentiate knowledge from thought.

---

32 Ibid., 49.

CONCLUSION

SONIC ENCOUNTERS AND POLITICAL STRUGGLES

There's an immense power that comes from hearing an explanation for one's oppression and our collective poverty and
misery. To know that it's not our fault, that it's not due to
individual choices or lifestyle habits but rather due to the very
dynamics of capitalism, dynamics that—as a *general absolute
law*—create an ever-expansive reserve army. Yet explanation is
only one part of the marxist pedagogical dialectic. The other
part—inquiry—is a different kind of power: the power of
wonder. Elizabeth Ellsworth insists that, "when taught and
used as a thing made, knowledge, the trafficked commodity
of educators and producers of educational media, becomes
nothing more than the decomposed by-product of something
that has already happened to us."[1] This is not a mere *epistemological* abstraction, but an *ontological* one as well insofar as we
experience ourselves as abstractions, as individuals. Ellsworth

---

1 Elizabeth Ellsworth, *Places of Learning: Media, Architecture, Pedagogy* (New York: Routledge, 2005), 1.

shows that pedagogy itself is differentializing and contingent, insofar as "the 'self' is what emerges from that learning experience... When my self and what I know are simultaneously in the making, my body/brain/mind is participating in an event that exists outside the realm of language."[2] The pedagogical experience is not about *knowledge* but about *thinking*, which is, in turn, about *thinking the limits of thought*. Ellsworth reminds us "that the very possibility of thought is predicated upon our opportunities and capacities to encounter the *limits* of thinking and knowing."[3]

If one side of the marxist pedagogical dialectic is about knowing and presentation, then we have to attend to the other side, which is about thought and inquiry. Such a distinction turns on the dialectic between exchange-value and use-value, between abstraction and differentialization, between capitalism and communism. The dialectic itself is here, in the present, in the global capitalist world, but in the world in transition. Understanding or knowing involves a determinate judgment that takes place when given data comes under the mind's order and comprehension is a faculty of determination in which data comes under the mind's comprehension. Thinking, by contrast, is an exposure to stupor, an experience with immeasurable concepts that the mind can never grasp. Capitalism in its flexibility can accommodate and capture all kinds of knowledge, even minoritarian ones. By examining the student rebellions of the mid-20th-century, Roderick Ferguson shows that the university is "an institution that *socializes*

2 Ibid., 2.

3 Ibid., 25.

state and capital into emergent articulations of difference."[4] The incorporation of difference not only blunts its oppositional force but also provides more energy to commodify. Thus, the task is not—or *not only*—to make knowledge less abstract but to move beyond knowledge into thought, a process through which we can experience elements of communism in the present and maybe even forge a collective that can finally annihilate abstract space, sound, and being.

Sound studies has recently emerged as an area with which educational scholarship can productively and innovatively intertwine in the interests of disinterpellative encounters. Consider, for example, Dominic Pettman's concept of the vox mundi, a concept he uses to refer to the voices of the world. He defines this term more carefully, specifying that it's "not a coherent, organic, quasi-spiritual gestalt but the sum total of cacophonous, heterogeneous, incommensurate, and unsynthesizable sounds of the postnatural world."[5] It is important to establish that the vox mundi is not a singular voice that speaks for all of the different existences of the world. Rather, it's a collective of all the different voices of the world simultaneously existing/collaborating to create a larger voice, similar to a choir—but one the mind cannot *grasp* or *understand* because its harmony is beyond thought's limits.

Applying this to marxist education, the vox mundi helps

---

4 Roderick Ferguson, *The Reorder of Things: The University and its Pedagogies of Minority Difference* (Minneapolis: University of Minnesota Press, 2012), 9.

5 Dominic Pettman, *Sonic Intimacy: Voice, Species, Technics* (Stanford: Stanford University Press, 2017), 8.

us move from understanding to thinking, from individuality to transindividual collectivity. "To posit a vox mundi," Pettman tells us, "is to do two important things: first, force us to reflect on what it is about our own voices that make us so confident in their exceptional status as bearer of 'humanity'; and oblige us to listen to the sound of the surround differently, more sympathetically and with greater nuance of attention which may encourage a more inclusive notion of what counts as having presence."[6] We're able to experience encounters more often because new differential sonic elements circulate and suspend our conceptions of the human as atomistic and, therefore, unique. As a vox mundi, the earth, animals, humans, digital networks, and more are transformed for a moment from forms of *capital* (raw materials, labor power, etc.) or knowledge sources and into *elements of communism* that we might encounter as we try to experience the present beyond that historical materialism intimates.

There's really no such thing as silence. As a result, I proffer that sight produces knowledge and understanding better than the ear, although it depends on our mode of listening. For marxists, the key is to move from hearing to listening, the former being an opening of the ear towards the known and the latter an opening of the ear toward the unknown and unexpected, or the "aural punctum," or that which "has the potential to create a glitch in the humanist machinery, when it surprises us with the intensity or force of an 'aural punctum'—a sonic prick or wound, which unexpectedly troubles

---

6 Ibid., 72.

our own smooth assumptions or untested delusions."[7] Building on Roland Barthes' visual punctum, the aural punctum "prick[s] up the ears." What is crucial is that it cannot be *known* because "what I can name cannot really prick me."[8] As a result, listening for the vox mundi opens us up to the aural punctum, moving us from understanding and real abstractions towards thinking and differentialized thinking and living.[9]

The Sounds of Anti-Colonial Struggles

Of course, the punctum's opening is not inherently progressive or revolutionary. As a result, the history of sonic rebellion in revolutionary struggles demonstrates the tight dialectic between inquiry and presentation, between synchrony and diachrony. In particular, Michael Denning's study of anticolonial phonographs during the electric revolution expands our understanding into considerations of nationality, imperialism, and race. Here, the technologies of the electric revolution worked to prefigure, inaugurate, and facilitate struggles against colonialism. Denning focuses in particular on the phonograph revolution in vernacular music in the 1920s, mostly between 1925 and the Great Depression. What he calls a "noise uprising" was located in and between, and facilitated by, the colonial ports. It thus took place in the Americas and Caribbean, Africa, Asia, the Pacific Islands, and elsewhere.

---

7 Ibid., 5.

8 Ibid., 46.

9 For more on listening and subjectivity, see Derek R. Ford, *Inhuman Educations: Jean-François Lyotard, Pedagogy, Thought* (Boston: Brill, 2021).

While we tend to think of original phonograph records as artifacts from *previous* musical cultures, these were squarely modern and contemporary. Moreover, they were fundamentally linked not only with Empire and imperialism, but with the emerging anti-imperialist and decolonial movements. He even suggests that they prefigured the political wave of decolonization in the 20th century. The capitalist mode of production not only abstracted the sonic environment and created a lo-fi atmosphere, but also worked to facilitate a counterrevolution of a hi-fi audible soundscape and attendant listening practices that upset the colonial harmonics of the era.

Capitalism, after all, was not just a European or Western development. Not only did it emerge in modern China, but even Marx's study of British capitalism was a *global* study; as his theory of value was a *global* theory from the start.[10] From its very origins, it was an international and internationalizing system. Marx's study showed how the interests of British workers and British colonialism were directly opposed. In the first volume of *Capital*, for example, he detailed how Ireland could be utilized for needed labor power and, in the third volume, he proposed that colonialism was one countervailing tendency

10 For China's early capitalist development, see Ken Hammond, "Beyond the Sprouts of Capitalism: China's Early Capitalist Development and Contemporary Socialist Project," *Liberation School*, 13 September 2021. Available here: https://liberationschool.org/beyond-the-sprouts-of-capitalism-understanding-chinas-contemporary-socialist-project.

for the rate of profit to fall.[11] And, of course, he ended volume 1 by writing how *British* capital originated—repeatedly—through "conquest, enslavement, robbery, murder," through national and international debts, the theft of gold and silver, "the enslavement and entombment in mines of the aboriginal population" and "the conquest and looting of the East Indies," among other "idyllic" processes.[12] And as Pradella demonstrates, Marx's analysis of colonialism not only made his theory of value possible, but Marx even located the potential sparks of British proletarian rebellion within anti-colonial struggles.[13] For example, in 1853 during the Taiping Uprising in China, Marx proposed that "it may safely be augured that the Chinese revolution will throw the spark into the overloaded mine of the present industrial system and cause the explosion of the long-prepared general crisis, which, spreading abroad, will be closely followed by political revolutions on the Continent."[14]

During the early 20th century, such sparks were sonic. The vernacular musics "emerged on the edges and borders of the

11 Karl Marx, *Capital: A Critique of Political Economy (Vol. 3): The Process of Capitalist Production as a Whole*, trans. D. Fernbach (New York: Penguin, 1894/1981), 345.

12 Karl Marx, *Capital (Vol. 1)*, 668, 703.

13 Pradella, *Globalisation and the Critique of Political Economy*.

14 Karl Marx, "Revolution in China and Europe," in *Marx and Engels Collected Works (Vol. 12): 1853-1854*, ed. J.S. Allen, P.S. Foner, D.J. Struik, and W.W. Weinstone (London: Lawrence & Wisehart, 1853/2010), 98.

empires of global capitalism, in the barrios, bidonvilles, barrack-yards, arrabels and favelas of an archipelago of colonial ports," which were "linked by steamship routes, railway lines, and telegraph cables, moving commodities and people across and between empires."[15] In other words, it was not a unidirectional top-down process of creating a new soundscape, but a dialectical engagement that facilitated resistance through new audible configurations and listening practices. The ports were particularly important, as they brought together and merged different peoples and cultures, creating soundscapes that "reverberated with sounds out of place, discordant noises."[16] In response to the standardization and abstraction of the industrial factory—and, as we've seen, of space and air and pedagogy—capitalism also facilitated "the dissemination of vernacular musics," which "together... created, not a 'world music,' but a radically new configuration of world musical space, a new musical world-system."[17] It was not uniform, and its challenge manifested precisely as noisy clashes.

The vernacular noise entailed two dominant phenomena: noisy timbres and syncopated rhythms. Regarding the first, because they were often the result of errant encounters of different peoples, the musics "usually combined instruments with distinct and often clashing timbres" which used both Western and Indigenous instruments. Thus, rather than seeing

---

15 Michael Denning, *Noise Uprising: The Audiopolitics of a World Revolution* (New York: Verso, 2015), 38.

16 Ibid., 40.

17 Ibid., 68.

the Western soundscape as imperialistic, we see an anticolonial reappropriation of instruments and thus a reconfiguration of that soundscape. Denning notes, for example, that Western instruments "became indigenous instruments," such that it no longer made sense to speak of the guitar as being a non-African musical device. Regarding the second, the music's use of syncopation, "a more or less technical term for the displacement of accents to the weak or off beat."[18] This caused significant disruptions and became not only an aesthetic but a political category.

Moreover, this sonic resistance also reversed the exportation of capital from the center to the periphery, as the phonograph records emanated in diverse pathways. Thus, even though the financial profits often emanated back to the imperial core, at the same time the capitalistic worldwide distribution helped to ignite the inspiring anti-colonial struggles of the mid-20th century. It was not the *content* of the message but the very form of it and how their "very sound disrupted the hierarchical orders and patterns of deference that structured colonial and settler societies," which "were heard as a violation of the musical order, an active challenge to the social 'harmony'" of the capitalist mode of production. [19] The sounds of capitalism and imperialism are not only unconfined to the sounds of weapons and machines, but even those sounds do not operate in a deterministic way.

At least in part, it was the anti-colonial noise uprising in tandem with the internal development of the capitalist mode

---

18 Ibid., 188.

19 Ibid., 155.

of production that brought about the need for a reconfiguration of sounding technologies and their filtration through digital conceptions of information and communication transmission. As the distinction between noise and sound is not internal to the properties or relations internal to either, both are social conceptions that change in response to political, economic, and social struggles. Thus, the bourgeoisie condemned the noise of the proletarian crowds of the late 19th and early 20th centuries while the progressive movements found inspiration and a new form of collective being by their participation within them.

As information and knowledge grew in importance for capitalism—and hence also for colonialism and imperialism—noise began to be defined as anything that would hinder production or that would limit or disable the effective transmission of inputs to outputs. In our increasingly "infocentric" society, noise is pitted against information. For Mack Hagood, infocentrism posits an ontology that naturalizes what it produces by figuring that "life is a battle for control between self-organizing information and the entropy that would dissolve it into noise."[20] One way this materialized in digital technologies was through AT&T's production of long-distance telephones. In order to reduce the noise of long-distance calls to maximize the information relayed, "the solution reached was to compress messages into a binary code that *eliminated all surplus*, leaving only the elements necessary to decompress the

---

20 Mack Hagood, *Hush: Media and Sonic Self-Control* (Durham: Duke University Press, 2019), 156.

full message at the output end."[21]

By the 1980s, when digital technologies began spreading in earnest in the music industry, the ability to convert musical signals into ones and zeros allowed for greater precision, attention to micro-details, and the elimination of background noise. When we hear music that's been digitally recorded, we hear "no noises accompanying them."[22] The silence of the sounds helped listeners acknowledge the previously unheard noise in musical recordings. Once we utilize these technologies, they train us in listening and hearing, so that we listen for—and as a result, hear—signals and codes rather than noise. To the extent that we listen for and hear noise, we do to eliminate it or—what may amount to the same thing—transform it into information.

It is possible to hear and listen to their sonic choreography in ways that unsettle assumptions of the clear boundaries between the human and machine and the link between the voice and an interior essence and, as a result, the perceptual biases that ontologically abstracted world and subjectivity. This is precisely where the liberatory potential of the vox mundi lies. Consider the autotuned voice. "When the voice is manipulated and takes on a mechanical or robotic sound, this link to the real 'self' of the singer is broken."[23] Since our dominant assumptions link the voice to a human essence—

---

21 Ibid., 156-157.

22 Ragnhild Brøvig-Hanssen and Anne Danielson, *Digital Signatures: The Impact of Digitalization on Popular Music Sound* (Cambridge: The MIT Press, 2016), 61.

23 Ibid., 128-129.

and thus deprive those without voices or whose voices are not heard to the status of agents—the overt autotuning of the voice continues to be controversial. Moreover, the autotuned voice is disturbing. When the voice as an assumed instrument linked to the interiority of the human is blended with the digital in such a way that, in Pettman's words, we realize that "there is something profoundly *im*personal about the voice, something alien."[24] The boundaries between the human and machine are blurred and the voice of each emerge with their limitations and potentials. It becomes impossible to tell where the machine ends and the human begins and, thus, where to locate the intelligence of the sound. This, in turn, destabilizes our conceptions of sound and the binary between sound and noise. This could represent an insurrection in the current ontological and epistemological regimes through which we encounter the swerve of atoms clashing and experience our potentiality to take power and transform the world through the transindividual collective power of the working and oppressed classes.

A Final Marxist Pedagogical Gesture

Althusser importantly reminds us that there is no linearity to marxism, and that when Lenin proposed that imperialism was the culminating stage of capitalism, he did not mean it would result in socialism. In fact, the "evolutionist representation of Marxist theory" is "yet another victory, and a big one, of bourgeois ideology."[25] We are still in the age of imperialism,

---

24 Pettman, *Sonic Agency*, 39.

25 Althusser, *History and Imperialism*, 121.

and the task at hand is to fight against it by waging class warfare in all arenas—including those of postdigital science and education.

In an oft-cited definition, the postdigital is defined as "hard to define; messy; unpredictable; digital and analog; technological and non-technological; biological and informational. The postdigital is both a rupture in our existing theories and their continuation."[26] The postdigital is a stupefying question or moment that demands we retune ourselves constantly, which is the same gesture that Marx makes, even in *Capital*, as the book is "a theoretical, systematic text, yet an unfinished … one … because it supposes a culmination … that is other than theoretical, an outside in which theory would be 'pursued by other means.'"[27] It demands experimentation, yet a kind of experimentation that capital cannot capture or enclose.

To return to a text discussed in the first chapter, one example of such an experiment would be *Reading Capital*, the book collectively authored by Althusser and his students. In his first contribution, Althusser begins by noting that the book is a series of notes from a seminar course and they "bear the mark of these circumstances: not only in their construction, their rhythm, their didactic or oral style, but above all in their discrepancies, the repetitions, hesitations and uncertain steps in their investigations."[28] They could have, he writes, tried

26 Petar Jandrić, Jeremy Knox, Tina Besley, Thomas Ryberg, Juha Souranta, and Sarah Hayes, "Postdigital Science and Education," *Educational Philosophy and Theory* 50, no. 10 (2018): 895.

27 Althusser, *History and Imperialism*, 144.

28 Althusser, "From *Capital* to Marx's Philosophy," 11.

"to make a *finished* work out of them," but chose instead "to present them for what they are: precisely, incomplete texts, the mere beginnings of a *reading*."[29] Toward the end of the contribution, Althusser notes that Marx develops concepts in two ways, synchronically and diachronically. Both are forms of presenting and producing knowledge that amount to learning, yet both have different scientific procedures and different *knowledge effects*.

"Synchrony," Althusser writes, "represents the organizational structure of the concepts in the thought-totality or *system*," while "diachrony [represents] the movement succession of the concepts in the ordered discourse of the proof."[30] When only read or written synchronically, concepts are presented linearly as building blocks for further concepts. Yet diachrony is when concepts are developed through displacement as they take on different contingencies and, as a result, *dislocate* knowledge. Each has a distinct temporality, as synchrony proceeds through succession linearly and according to a developmental logic while diachrony is open and aleatory, uncertain and hesitant.

We can grasp the pedagogical simultaneity of the synchronic and diachronic through two recent theorizations of Althusser's pedagogy, both of which build on Althusser's notion of interpellation. For Althusser, ideology functions concretely through interpellation, a process through which we are

---

29 Ibid.

30 Ibid., 70.

"recruited" into the dominant ideology.[31] David Backer gives an example from his school life: when he received his state test scores. Backer writes that his father "said that if I didn't score higher on such tests in the future, then I wouldn't be allowed to go to summer camp… the test interpellated me in this case: I learned that I had to behave in a certain way with these tests, that around here we perform well on state tests, or else."[32] For Althusser—and this is important—there is no "temporal succession" of interpellation: "ideology has always-already in-terpellated individuals as subjects."[33] Even before we're born, we're given a name, interpellated into a lineage, and so on. The ideological state apparatuses (like the school, church, family, media, and so on) function along with the repressive state apparatuses (like the police, army, courts, and so on). Althusser saw the school as becoming the dominant ideological state apparatus. Thus, the *content* of schooling matters less than the *form* of schooling. In Backer's case, what the test tested was of less concern than the testing process itself.

Interpellation is significant because it moves the class struggle into the realm of ideology and theory. What happens

---

31 What might be less well known is that *one* of Althusser's pur-poses in developing the theory of interpellation is to agitate against anti-socialist theories or "anticipatory" works depicting "totalitar-ian" socialist society as a society in which every individual will be doubled by his personal "monitor." See Louis Althusser, *On the Reproduction of Capitalism*, ed. J. Bidet, trans. B. Brewster and G.M. Goshgarian (New York: Verso, 2014), 177.

32 Backer, *The Gold and the Dross*, 6.

33 Althusser, *On the Reproduction of Capitalism*, 192.

in schools is thus central because it can determine "the balance of power in the class struggle… *in the number-one Ideological State Apparatus*."[34] Interpellation is the glue that fastens the contradictory and antagonistic modes of production in any given social formation—including their social relations—together. Glue, of course, does not always hold, never permanently seals anything, and cannot conquer the air. As such, interpellation does not fully succeed, and we can pedagogically facilitate such failures through multiple means, the first of which is counterinterpellation.

Backer defines counterinterpellation as "a taking up and taking on those interpellations that shift the balance of forces away from the ruling class's control."[35] Counterinterpellation is a refusal of interpellation, a rejection of the hailing that positions the subject within the reproduction of capitalist relations. Counterinterpellation acknowledges and militates against such practices in the production of antagonistic subjectivities. Interpellations are "small moments with big meanings: they are the concrete practical moments whereby social context weaves through consciousness, connecting with and composing individual subjectivity."[36] Yet interpellations are never secured and are fragile, subject to the class struggle. For example, we're interpellated into and through language but return and utilize language "in undeniably unique ways,"

---

34 Ibid., 159.

35 David I. Backer, "Interpellation, Counterinterpellation, and Education," *Critical Education* 9, no. 15 (2018): 11.

36 Ibid., 5.

such as through "poetry, innuendo, paradox, neologism, philosophy, and puns" which "all happen within and against the prefabricated linguistic structures speakers must speak."[37] I remember someone shouting "queer" at a friend and me as we were walking down the street, and my friend responding with a loud "thank you"! This was a refusal of an attempted interpellation of us into abject subjects and a counterinterpellation that affirmed a different sense of queerness.

As we saw earlier, for Lewis the marxist philosophy *internal* to marxist politics is disinterpellation, the force of the swerve of atoms. For Lewis, counterinterpellation is a political practice that is always oriented in a particular direction and therefore is not properly educational. The disinterpellative encounter produces a "relationship between actors and the world is not fixed or determined in advance. Instead, the very conditions for a different world open up, as in Althusser's reading of Machiavelli wherein an unknown man in an unknown place."[38] A marxist—and hence historical-materialist—pedagogy "exposes the student to the clash of atoms, which destabilizes and suspends any and every interpellative process to open the subject to that "which is beyond subjectivity: a revolutionary being-in-common that is a precondition for a different kind of world."[39] Counterinterpellation for Lewis is still too tethered to *this* world, and blocks encounters with the unknown and the desubjectified subject—or the col-

---

37 Ibid., 9.

38 Lewis, "A Marxist Education of the Encounter," 316.

39 Ibid.

lective transindividual common of the many.

One problem Backer identifies with disinterpellation is that "it assumes a moment beyond ideology but really is predicated on "an ideology with certain features, namely that of a communist horizon."[40] As a result, there is still an unacknowledged political project and orientation at play. For Backer, the marxist teacher works to produce counterinterpellation through "knowing what kinds of social forces act on and through one's classroom' and helping 'students learn how to make interventions that shift the social formation's balance of forces."[41] For Lewis, on the other hand, counterinterpellation is a political necessity but one that does not allow for the educational experience of making "the subject unfamiliar to itself and thus open to its own dissolution through the encounter with an outside."[42] The marxist teacher cannot *make* such an experience happen but can only try to "open a space for an encounter by setting up the possibilities for a clash" and holding onto such clashes.[43] Counterinterpellation necessitates the teacher's knowledge, while disinterpellation necessitates the subject's openness to non-knowledge.

I propose that the pedagogical interplay of synchrony and diachrony allows for the play of both disinterpellation and counterinterpellation. It is not that the teacher *does not* have

---

40 Backer, "Interpellation, Counterinterpellation, and Education," 16.

41 Ibid., 19.

42 Lewis, "A Marxist Education of the Encounter," 314.

43 Ibid.

a politics—as if that was possible—or that capitalist forces
like debt cease operating on the student's subjectivity. On the
contrary, the student who suffers the aleatory swerve is in a
state of *deferral* while disinterpellated. The void, after all, is still
composed of *matter* as "something cannot come from nothing."[44] This deferral is a decomposition of individual capitalist
subjectivity, a *feeling* that the collectivization of the proletarian
class is realizable. On the other hand, counterinterpellation is
the political experience of intervening to produce that collective and advance the class struggle. Counterinterpellation is a
synchronic movement that shifts the balance of forces by as-
serting a revolutionary knowledge and subject position against
capitalism, while disinterpellation is a diachronic movement
that reveals the limitations of revolutionary knowledge and
subjectivity under capitalism. In neither case do we renounce,
as Althusser puts it, "that it is possible to organize the workers'
class struggle for the seizure of power and for socialism."[45]
The pedagogical mode is one in which the synchronic and
diachronic dialectically intertwine as—and with—the digital
and analog.

In their *application* of these scientific procedures, David
Kristjanson-Gural argues that neither can be used without the
other without producing errors. The "synchronic error is the
failure to take into account the effect of new contingencies
on the meaning of the terms within the logical totality at a
given moment or level of abstraction," while the "diachronic

---

44 Goshgarian, "The Void of the Forms of Historicity as Such,"
245.

45 Althusser, *History and Imperialism*, 155.

error results from comparing logical claims at two different moments or levels of analysis without taking into around the different meanings and relationships between concepts that apply at each level."[46] Kristjanson-Gural shows that the synchronic error results in the very notion that Marx leaves us with a "transformation problem" (e.g., Marx cannot account for the transformation of value into price), and the diachronic error results in a total rejection that supply and demand *simultaneously* "both cannot and must directly affect the value of commodities" because both contradictory claims "belong to distinct stages in the expansion of the logical totality."[47] *Both* errors occur when *only* one pedagogical logic is applied; thus the key to Althusser's reading of *Capital* insists on the dialectical and contingent or tactical deployment of presentation and inquiry. This is why Marx himself blocks them together and never claims to present a unified and ahistorical theory, science, philosophy, or practice.

The pedagogical force of their simultaneity is that of a rupture in the world as it is: both knowledge and non-knowledge, information and ignorance, a step forward and sideways. One reads the book and understands-learns the content while remaining stupefied in the face of its potential meaning. Counterinterpellations on their own can potentially produce new knowledge commons for capital to expropriate, or they can produce disinterpellative experiences in that the refusal of the insult of interpellation opens a space for the encounter

46 David Kristjanson-Gural, "Poststructural Logic in Marx's Theory of Value," *Rethinking Marxism* 21, no. 1 (2009): 15.

47 Ibid., 28.

with another possible world and set of social relations that we cannot *know* in the present but can only *feel*.

The pedagogical directive is to *inhabit* this heterogeneity in the face of capital's all-powerful forces of abstraction. We experience a collectivity but, more pointedly, a collectivity that remains mute and infantile *and* antagonistic and public. The political project is, then, to force these encounters to cohere so that we can build communism, sublating the relationship between what is now antagonistically divided between fixed capital and living labor into a liberated, collective, ecological subject. Consider, by way of conclusion, digital technologies that mediate the voice through automatic tuning, filters, and other means. Such mediations reveal that vocalization is a "process without a subject" insofar as they prevent us from linking the sound of a voice to an essence of an individual subject *or* a piece of fixed capital. They produce another sonic surplus that capital *might* capture if we only listen synchronically for new meanings and knowledges or that workers *might* utilize for oppositional counterinterpellations. But if we listen diachronically as well, we receive an immersive education in the *wonder* as well as the *theory* of class struggle, a struggle that is advanced ideologically and materially through the forces of opposition and swerve. This is a politics that refuses to articulate a program that capital could accommodate or even understand.

The alternative is a silence that we also find in Marx, but what I have in mind here is what Marx leaves us with in the third volume of *Capital*, which as Althusser reminds us, ends

with "a title: *Classes*. Forty lines, then silence."[48] It's a silence
that *inhabits* the form of the writing's end, one silence inaugu-
rated not by death but by the very indeterminacy of Marx's
work, the openness of marxist pedagogy, and the promise of
marxist philosophy and the class struggle.

---

48 Louis Althusser, "Marx's Immense Theoretical Revolution," in
Reading Capital, 349.

BIBLIOGRAPHY

Althusser, Louis. *For Marx*. Trans. B. Brewster. New York: Verso, 1965/2005.

Althusser, Louis. "From *Capital* to Marx's Philosophy." In L. Althusser, É. Balibar, R. Establet, P. Macherey, and J. Rancière, *Reading Capital*. Trans. B. Brewster and D. Fernbach. New York: Verso, 1965/2015.

Althusser, Louis. *History and Imperialism: Writings, 1963-1986*. Trans. G.M. Goshgarian. Cambridge: Polity Press, 2020.

Althusser, Louis. "Marx's Immense Theoretical Revolution." In L. Althusser, É. Balibar, R. Establet, P. Macherey, and J. Rancière, *Reading Capital*. Trans. B. Brewster and D. Fernbach. New York: Verso, 1965/2015.

Althusser, Louis. *On the Reproduction of Capitalism*. Ed. J. Bidet. Trans. B. Brewster and G.M. Goshgarian. New York: Verso, 2014

Althusser, Louis. *Philosophy for Non-Philosophers*. Trans. G.M. Goshgarian. London: Bloomsbury, 2017.

Althusser, Louis. *Philosophy of the Encounter: Later Writings, 1978-1987*. Trans. G.M. Goshgarian. New York: Verso, 2006.

Althusser, Louis. *The Humanist Controversy and Other Writings*.
Ed. F. Matheron. Trans. G.M. Goshgarian. New York:
Verso, 2003.

Backer, David I. "Interpellation, Counterinterpellation, and
Education." *Critical Education* 9, no. 15 (2018): 1-15.

Backer, David I. *The Gold and the Dross: Althusser for Educators*.
Boston: Brill, 2019.

Brennan, Teresa. *The Transmission of Affect*. Ithaca: Cornell
University Press, 2004.

Britton, Celia. "Globalization and Political Action in the
Work of Édouard Glissant." *Small Axe* 13, no. 3 (2009):
1-11.

Brøvig-Hanssen, Ragnhild and Anne Danielson, *Digital
Signatures: The Impact of Digitalization on Popular Music Sound*.
Cambridge: The MIT Press, 2016.

Dean, Jodi. *Crowds and Party*. New York: Verso, 2016.

Dean, Jodi. "Faces as Commons: The Secondary Visuality
of Communicative Capitalism." *Open!* 31 December 2016.
Available at: https://onlineopen.org/faces-as-commons.

Denning, Michael. *Noise Uprising: The Audiopolitics of a World
Revolution*. New York: Verso, 2015.

Detloff, Dean and Matt Bernico. "Atmoterrorism and At
modesign in the 21st Century: Mediating Flint's Water
Crisis." *Cosmos and History: The Journal of Natural and Social
Philosophy* 13, no. 1 (2017): 156-189.

Ellsworth, Elizabeth. *Places of Learning: Media, Architecture,
Pedagogy*. New York: Routledge, 2005.

Ferguson, Roderick. *The Reorder of Things: The University and
its Pedagogies of Minority Difference*. Minneapolis: University
of Minnesota Press, 2012.

Ford, Derek R. *Communist Study: Education for the Commons*, 2nd ed. Lanham: Lexington Books, 2021.

Ford, Derek R. *Inhuman Educations: Jean-François Lyotard, Pedagogy, Thought*. Boston: Brill, 2021.

Ford, Derek R. *Marxism, Pedagogy, and the General Intellect: Beyond the Knowledge Economy*. New York: Palgrave Macmillan.

Ford, Derek R. and Tyson E. Lewis. "On the Freedom to be Opaque Monsters: Communist Pedagogy, Aesthetics, and the Sublime." *Cultural Politics* 14, no. 1 (2018): 95-108.

Glissant, Édouard. *Poetics of Relation*. Tans. B. Wing. Ann Arbor: The University of Michigan Press, 1997.

Goshgarian, G.M. "The Void of the Forms of Historicity as Such." *Rethinking Marxism* 31, no. 3 (2019): 243-272.

Hagood, Mack. *Hush: Media and Sonic Self-Control*. Durham: Duke University Press, 2019.

Hammond, Ken. "Beyond the Sprouts of Capitalism: China's Early Capitalist Development and Contemporary Socialist Project." *Liberation School*, 13 September 2021. Available here: https://liberationschool.org/beyond-the-sprouts-of-capitalism-understanding-chinas-contemporary-socialist-project.

Han, Byung-Chul. *The Transparency Society*. Stanford: Stanford University Press, 2015.

Harootunian, Harry. *Marx After Marx: History and Time in the Expansion of Capitalism*. New York: Columbia University Press, 2015.

Hardt, Michael and Antonio Negri. *Assembly*. New York: Oxford University Press, 2017.

Harvey, David. *The Limits to Capital*. New York: Verso, 1982/2007.

Hobsbawm, Eric J. "Introduction." In K. Marx, *Pre-Capitalist Economic Foundations*. Ed. E.J. Hobsbawm. Trans. J. Cohen. New York: International Publishers, 1964.

Jandrić, Petar, Jeremy Knox, Tina Besley, Thomas Ryberg, Juha Souranta, and Sarah Hayes. "Postdigital Science and Education." *Educational Philosophy and Theory* 50, no. 10 (2018): 893-899.

Kristjanson-Gural, David. "Poststructural Logic in Marx's Theory of Value." *Rethinking Marxism* 21, no. 1 (2009): 14-33.

Lenin, V.I. "What is to be Done?" In *Essential Works of Lenin*. Ed. H.M. Christman. New York: Dover Publications, 1987.

Leupin, Alexandre. "The Slave's *Jouissance*." *Callaloo* 36, no. 4 (2013): 890-901.

Lewis, Tyson E. "A Marxist Education of the Encounter: Althusser, Interpellation, and the Seminar," *Rethinking Marxism* 29, no. 2 (2017): 303-317.

Lewis, Tyson E. "Mapping the Constellation of Educational Marxism(s)." *Educational Philosophy and Theory* 44, no. s1 (2012): 98-114.

Lewis, Tyson E. *On Study: Giorgio Agamben and Educational Potentiality*. New York: Routledge, 2013.

Lewis, Tyson E. "Afterword: Studying the Dross. In D. Backer, *The Gold and the Dross: Althusser for Educators*, Boston: Brill, 2019.

Lewis, Tyson E. "The Pedagogical Unconscious: Rethinking Marxist Pedagogy through Louis Althusser and Fredric Jameson." *Journal for Critical Education Policy Studies* 3, no. 2 (2005): 141-157.

Lewis, Tyson E. and Daniel Friedrich. "Educational States of

Suspension." *Educational Philosophy and Theory* 48, no. 3 (2016): 237-250.

Lyotard, Jean-François. *Postmodern Fables*. Trans. G.V.D. Abbeele. Minneapolis: University of Minnesota Press, 1993/1997.

Lyotard, Jean-François. *Soundproof Room: Malraux's Anti-Aesthetics*. Trans. R. Harvey. Stanford: Stanford University Press, 1993/2001.

Lyotard, Jean-François. *The Inhuman: Reflections on Time*. Trans. G. Bennington and R. Bowlby. Stanford: Stanford University Press, 1988/1991.

Lyotard, Jean-François. *The Postmodern Explained: Correspondence 1982-1985*. Trans. D. Barry, B. Maher, J. Pefanis, V. Spate, and M. Thomas. Minneapolis: University of Minnesota Press, 1988/1993.

Malott, Curry S. *A History of Education for the Many: From Colonization and Slavery to the Decline of US Imperialism*. London: Bloomsbury, 2021.

Malott, Curry S. "Capitalism, Crisis, and Educational Struggle in the Postdigital." *Postdigital Science and Education* 1, no. 2 (2019): 371-390.

Marcy, Sam. *High Tech, Low Pay: A Marxist Analysis of the Changing Character of the Workign Class*. New York: World View Forum, 2009.

Marx, Karl. *Capital: A Critique of Political Economy (Vol. 1): The Process of Capitalist Production*. Trans. S. Moore and E. Aveling. New York: International Publishers, 1867/1967.

Marx, Karl. *Capital: A Critique of Political Economy (Vol. 2): The Process of Circulation of Capital*. New York: International Publishers, 1885/1967.

Marx, Karl. *Capital: A Critique of Political Economy (Vol. 3): The Process of Capitalist Production as a Whole*. Trans. D. Fernbach. New York: Penguin, 1884/1981.

Marx, Karl. *Grundrisse: Foundations of the Critique of Political Economy (Rough Draft)*. Trans. M. Nicolaus. New York: Penguin Books, 1939/1993.

Marx, Karl. "Marx to Joseph Weydemeyer." In *Marx and Engels Collected Works (Vol. 39): Letters 1852-1855*. Ed. J.S. Allen, P.S. Foner, D.J. Struik, and W.W. Weinstone. London: Lawrence & Wisehart, 1852/2010.

Marx, Karl. "Revolution in China and Europe." In *Marx and Engels Collected Works (Vol. 12): 1853-1854*. Ed. J.S. Allen, P.S. Foner, D.J. Struik, and W.W. Weinstone. London: Lawrence & Wisehart, 1853/2010.

Marx, Karl and Friedrich Engels. "Marx and Engels to August Bebel, Wilhelm Liebknecht, Wilhelm Bracke and Others (Circular Letter)." Trans. P. Ross and B. Ross. In *Marx and Engels Collected Works (Vol. 45): Letters 1874-1879*. Ed. J.S. Allen, P.S. Foner, D.J. Struik. London: Lawrence & Wisehart, 1879/2010.

Marx, Karl and Friedrich Engels. *The German Ideology: Part One, with Selections from Parts Two and Three and Supplementary Texts*. Trans. C.J. Arthur. New York: International Publishers, 1932/1970.

Merrifield, Andy. *Marx Dead and Alive: Reading* Capital *in Precarious Times*. New York: Monthly Review Press, 2020.

Mitchell, Don. *The Right to the City: Social Justice and the Fight for Public Space*. New York: The Guilford Press, 2003.

Murdoch, H. Aldai. "Édouard Glissant's Creolized World Vision: From Resistance to Relation to *Opacité*." *Callaloo* 36, no. 4 (2013): 875-889.

Negri, Antonio. *Marx beyond Marx: Lessons on the Grundrisse.* Trans. H. Cleaver, M. Ryan, and M. Viano. New York: Autonomedia, 1979/1992.

Nesbitt, Nick. "Early Glissant: From the Destitution of the Political to Antillean Ultra-Leftism." *Callaloo* 36, no. 4 (2013): 932-948.

Pettman, Dominic. *Sonic Intimacy: Voice, Species, Technics.* Stanford: Stanford University Press, 2017.

Pradella, Lucia. *Globalisation and the Critique of Political Economy: New Insights from Marx's Writings.* New York: Routledge, 2016.

Read, Jason. *The Politics of Transindividuality.* Chicago: Haymarket Books, 2015.

Sloterdijk, Peter. *Spheres II: Globes: Macrosphereology.* Trans. W. Hoban. Los Angeles: Semiotext(e), 1999/2014.

Sloterdijk, Peter. *Spheres III: Foams: Plural Sphereology.* Trans. W. Hoban. Los Angeles: Semiotext(e), 2004/2016.

Starosta, Guido. "The System of Machinery and Determinations of Revolutionary Subjectivity in the *Grundrisse* and *Capital*." In *In Marx's Laboratory: Critical Interpretations of the Grundrisse.* Ed. R. Bellofiore, G. Starosta, and P.D. Thomas. Rotterdam: Brill, 2013.

Virno, Paolo. *Convention and Materialism.* Trans. L. Chiesa. Cambridge: The MIT Press, 1986/2020.

Willinsky, John. *Learning to Divide the World: Education at Empire's End.* Minneapolis: University of Minnesota Press, 1998.

Zhao, Weili. "Calibrating *Study* and *Learning* as Hermeneutic Principles through Greco-Christian Seeing, Rabbinic

Hearing, and Chinese *Yijing* Observing." *Studies in Philosophy and Education* 39, no. 3 (2020): 321-336.